"It's so hard to balance love and discipline when our kids are making poor choices. But Bonding with Your Teen through Boundaries is helping to make it a little easier. With a 'how-to' practicality, June Hunt helps parents tackle the hardest problems their kids face on the road to adulthood."

JOSH MCDOWELL
AUTHOR AND SPEAKER

"June Hunt's clear wisdom accumulated through two decades of interactive talk radio exudes through every page of this wonderful and much-needed book. The twenty-first century teenagers are crying for the fruit of this message. The discerning parent who reads and applies the wisdom found herein will undoubtedly save their kids from hurt, tears, and potential destruction."

JOE WHITE
PRESIDENT, KANAKUK KAMPS

J U N E   H U N T

Founder of Hope for the Heart Ministries

Bonding with Your Teen through Boundaries

BROADMAN
&HOLMAN
PUBLISHERS

Nashville, TN

0-8054-2452-0

Published by Broadman & Holman Publishers
Nashville, Tennessee

Dewey Decimal Classification: 649
Subject Heading: PARENT AND TEENAGER
Library of Congress Card Catalog Number: 2001035685

Library of Congress Cataloging-in-Publication Data
Hunt, June.
   Bonding with your teen through boundaries / June Hunt.
     p. cm.
  ISBN 0-8054-2452-0 (pb.)
  1. Parent and teenager. 2. Parent and teenager—Religious aspects—Christianity. 3. Parenting. 4. Discipline of children. I. Title.

HQ799.15 .H86   2001
649'.125—dc21

               2001035685
                   CIP

1 2 3 4 5 6 7 8 9 10 05 04 03 02 01

This book is dedicated to the delightfully endearing, fun-filled young people in my life—my nieces and nephews—who, God bless them, will one day have teenagers of their own.

Ashlee, Heather, Henry, Hunter I,
Hunter II, Josh, Kathryn, Kimberly, Leah,
Lillian, Mara, Tanner, Teddy, and Travis

My prayer is that you will always be young in spirit, pure in heart, and right with God.

ACKNOWLEDGMENTS

With deepest gratitude to the team who executed like true Super Bowl champions:

Barbara Spruill and Trudie Jackson who presented the game plan from their years of working with teens and without whom there would be no book.

Gary Terashita, my publisher and coach, who never lost faith in this project, although I certainly gave him cause.

Robin Hardy who ran with the game plan by compiling transcripts and writing life into the book.

Connie Steindorf who, quarter after quarter, ran with blazing fingers across the computer keyboard.

Kay Deakins who was the "front line" all by herself, and ran interference.

June Page who organized, researched, and wrote, making sure the ball wasn't dropped in the fourth quarter.

Beth Stapleton, Karen Williams, and Ann Redder who together, with bleary eyes, proofed the book across the end line as the game clock ran out.

CONTENTS

THE TUG OF WAR WITH TEENS

Tug of War. How well I remember the game! A line drawn in the dirt . . . two teams on opposite sides . . . a long, thick rope . . . each kid with both hands tightly gripping the rope. My team struggles and strains to pull every person on the other team across the line.

Who won the tug of war? The *taller, stronger* team, right? Although "taller and stronger" would *seem* to be the winning combination, that wasn't always so. The *real* winner was the team with the most leverage. Position and strategy could actually defeat a physically stronger team. Leaning at an angle away from the opposition and digging your heels into the dirt would many times make the difference.

Have you felt as if you've been in a tug of war with your teenager? You've established the boundary line and said with firmness, "I'm serious. This is not a game!" Nevertheless, this once-compliant child now angles away from you—with heels dug in deep. The tough-guy attitude communicates, "No way you'll get me to your side."

What do you do if you don't want to be in a tug of war, if you don't want to do battle? Do you withdraw and let your teen win? Although you may literally be taller and stronger, your teenager can exert a lot of leverage with clever tactics—tactics such as causing a family crisis, embarrassing you in front of your friends, sullying the family name.

Many a parent has indeed cried "uncle" and given up their role as "parent." They've also given up establishing appropriate rules, thinking, *I can't win anyway, and I need to have some kind of relationship. Maybe we can be friends. I'll give up the rules to salvage the relationship.*

While the emphasis on "relationship" sounds noble, if you abdicate your position as parent, what kind of relationship can you have? Your teenagers may have been born at night but not last night! They know that parents are responsible for establishing rules—boundary lines—and that crossing the line brings repercussions. So, when you withdraw from the rightful role of "boundary setter," your teen feels *superior*—and views you as *inferior.* Because your withdrawal makes you look emotionally weak, your teen feels emotionally strong. So now with this new empowerment—"I've won the tug of war!"—comes the self-centered assumption, "I have the right to rebel."

The purpose of this book is to help you win—not a war but *a relationship of mutual respect.* It may take a long time—possibly months, possibly years. But remember, a passive parent never wins respect. Neither does an oppressive parent. My prayer is that you, in your rightful parenting role, will be able to *bond* with your teen *through boundaries*—boundaries with appropriate repercussions and rewards, boundaries that instill self-control and success—and that, in the end, you both will win!

Each day ask for the Lord's supernatural wisdom and commit your parenting to Him.

Commit to the LORD whatever you do,
and your plans will succeed.
PROVERBS 16:3

WHAT ARE BOUNDARIES ALL ABOUT?

CHAPTER 1
PREPARE YOUR KITE
FOR FLIGHT

Teenagers are a hot topic. One writer lamented: "They now seem to love luxury; they have bad manners and contempt for authority; they show disrespect for adults and spend their time hanging around places gossiping with one another. They are ready to contradict their parents, monopolize the conversation and company, eat gluttonously and tyrannize their teachers. . . ." Not much has changed since Socrates made these complaints some twenty-four hundred years ago.

Immediately after college, I became intimately acquainted with those turbulent teenage years—the time of tremendous change—as a youth director in a large downtown church. I had six hundred in the junior high division, grades seven, eight, and nine. It didn't take long to learn that between ages thirteen and sixteen, teenagers came in like lambs—and went out like lions. I not only marveled at the changes, but also gained invaluable insights. Many of those practical insights are shared within the pages of this book.

For example, in the earliest years of your child's life, you as a parent represented God—and I mean that literally. You represented total authority. You were always right. Then your teenager entered into this time of "individualization"—that fifty-dollar word describing the stage of development when children strive to become independent young persons. No longer do they simply accept your morals, values, and teachings based on *"just because I said so!"* Teenagers want—and actually need—to recognize and respond to those truths for themselves or else they could find themselves sliding down a dangerously slippery slope. That is why Proverbs 4:14–16 gives this clear caution: "Do not set foot on the path of the wicked or walk in the way of evil men. Avoid it, do not tread on it; turn from it and go on your way. For they cannot sleep till they do evil; they are robbed of slumber till they make someone fall." If teenagers don't heed this warning, they will end up following *anyone* at *anytime* for *any reason*—especially any so-called authority who comes along with a message that sounds good, whether it be drug dealer, cult leader, or gang lord.

Unfortunately for parents, this new push for independence is not usually a gradual transition. Your kids hit the teen years and PRESTO CHANGE-O!—all of a sudden Mom knows nothing and Dad is a dinosaur. Their attitude is: "My parents must have been born in the Stone Age!"

During this time of tug of war, teenagers will test you, tempt you, try you. In other words, they're trying to see if there are any *real* rules. Many parents become baffled by their teens' behavior, thinking, *What happened to my obedient son? Who is this difficult daughter? How do I deal with this awful attitude?*

If something similar is happening in your home, take heart: *Now is not forever.* One day you may be surprised to see that your teenager has grown to be an appreciative adult who finally hears your heart and sees your sacrifices. Until that time, however—*hold on to hope.*

In a way, kids are like kites. (I'm fully aware that some adults object to using the word *kid* for a young person because *kid* literally means a young goat. However, I affectionately use the word *kid* as a term of endearment—probably because it's casual, and kids like most things to be casual.)

Speaking of kites and kids, I can still picture a large Thanksgiving gathering at my mother's home. When I walked outside, I noticed a kite on the ground, a kite obviously discarded in frustration. The string was knotted into a huge, oddly shaped ball. A few relatives joined me in wanting to fly the kite, but we didn't have any other string. So for twenty minutes or more, three of us stood around the kite untangling the knots one at a time. The process was slow and tedious. But when the tangles were untied, the kite was put to flight. At first it ascended into the air to our smiles, laughter, and cheers. It then abruptly descended in a nose dive and hit the ground. That downfall, however, did not dash our hopes. After several more unsuccessful launches, the kite again was put to flight—and oh, how it soared!

Just because many teens are all tied up in knots doesn't mean that they should be treated like discards. Just because they've fallen to the ground doesn't mean they are hopelessly defeated. To untangle a mess takes persistence and patience. Be encouraged by this compassionate principle from the Bible: "A man's wisdom gives him patience; it is to his glory to overlook an offense" (Prov. 19:11).

To be the best parent possible, you must have persistence and patience while being guided by the right goal.

A Parent's Highest Goal

Our ultimate goal as parents is to prepare our "kites" for flight so that they can be all that the "Kite Maker" intended. Simply put: *prepare your child to live independently of you, successfully soaring with self-control.* This self-control will not be misdirected when it is grounded by the Word of God, governed by the Son of God, and guided by the Spirit of God.

By God's design you have been placed in a key position to prepare your kite for flight. How?

Four Key Points—for Kites *and* Kids

1. Kites need open spaces in order to soar; they will be hindered by hovering tree limbs. As a parent, be open with your teen and don't hover.

2. Kites need to be attached to a firmly-held ball of string. They will plummet to the ground if you let go completely. As a parent, don't let go of your teens. Even when they make it difficult, stay connected. Keep holding on, giving them love—keep holding on, giving them limits.

3. Kites need for the string to be released more and more in order to soar higher and higher. As your kids take on increased responsibility, don't fear giving them increased freedom.

4. Kites need balance. The weight of the tail balances the kite, keeping it from flip-flopping. If you find yourself being accused of weighting your teenager down, don't despair—your teenager needs *balance through boundaries*.

If you really care about your kids, learn how to present boundaries with both repercussions and rewards. Teenagers will be far more balanced with boundaries, and in the end you will see them soar!

CHAPTER 2
THE BLACK HAT

To the fascination of the watching world, the early 1900s ushered in the first motion pictures in black and white. Western films were popular fare as the two main characters—the hero and the villain—shot it out with their six-shooters.

In the old Westerns, it didn't take any time to discover which was the *good guy* and which was the *bad guy.* The good guy always wore the white hat. The bad guy always wore the black. Everyone liked the hero in the white hat. No one liked the villain in the black hat.

But I Don't Want to Wear the Black Hat

And so it goes in the family. No parent wants to be villainized; no dad wants to be disliked; no mom wants to be disrespected. Every parent wants to be liked and listened to with respect. So what do you do if your teenager deliberately crosses the line of disobedience—and you don't want to wear "the black hat"?

Some parents assume that the solution is *permissiveness:* permit children to do whatever they want to do (often against the parents' better judgment) so that the children will not be upset and the family can live in peace. No reprimand, no reproach, no repercussion. For the child who chooses to cross the line, no negative consequence. Unfortunately, this style of parenting provides no solution. This passive tactic—"peace at any price"—will *not* reap the positive results that every parent desires. You want to raise a self-disciplined young person who respects both your role as a parent and your right to set the rules!

Isn't "Peace at Any Price" the Way Jesus Lived?

Many people—Christians and non-Christians alike—feel that "peace at any price" is the Christian way to live. "After all," they reason, "Jesus is known as the Prince of Peace." They may even quote Jesus, who said, "Blessed are the peacemakers" (Matt. 5:9) and "My peace I give you" (John 14:27). And it's true, even the apostle Paul said, "If it is possible, as far as it depends on you, live at peace with everyone" (Rom. 12:18).

In light of—or in spite of—all these biblical passages, we need to ask ourselves, "Was Jesus a peace-at-any-price person?" By no means. Instead, He countered this common misconception by pronouncing, "I did not come to bring peace, but a sword" (Matt. 10:34). Jesus clearly communicated that at times He must confront what is wrong by cutting to the heart of the matter. He announced that "the truth will set you free" (John 8:32).

At certain times, the sword of truth is necessary to live a life of integrity and confront needed changes. When you do what is right in His sight, Jesus will give you His supernatural peace. Although everything around you is not peaceful, He can give you an internal peace that passes all understanding.

How does this happen? When you receive Jesus Christ into your heart as your personal Lord and Savior, He comes in to take control of your heart and life. Because He is the Prince of Peace, *He will be peace* for you. He will be your peace in the midst of the storm—even a stormy time with your teenager. But having the peace of Christ on the inside is entirely different from being a peace-at-any-price person.

What Happens If You Are a Peace-at-Any-Price Parent?

Recently, two young people told me that their parents had been "too permissive." One fifteen-year-old boy confided,

"My mother doesn't want to tell me no, and my stepfather just gets mad at Mom because she backs down on limits she sets."

The other young person, an attractive twenty-year-old admitted, "When I was much younger, I never should have been permitted to stay out as late as I did. And I never should have been permitted to be with certain men—they were much too old for me. My parents didn't check to see what was going on . . . and it wasn't good. Now that I'm on my own, I've had real difficulties setting and keeping my own personal boundaries."

Both of these young people shared that they didn't think their parents cared enough about them. They thought their parents were too busy or too preoccupied to set appropriate boundaries. And both of them will admit that they have acted angrily and disrespectfully toward their parents.

In reality, if you "permit" your teens to transgress the line, three primary problems will surface:

1. They will disrespect the appropriate rules.
2. They will dismiss their own need for self-discipline.
3. They will disregard your role and your right to parent them.

Ultimately, passive parenting will dramatically decrease respect for you as a parent.

So, what do you do when you know you shouldn't be a peace-at-any-price parent, but at the same time you don't want to go to war . . . you don't want to be overbearing . . . you don't want to wear *the black hat?*

You need to learn the benefit of boundaries.

What Are Boundaries?

Boundaries are *established limits*—lines not to be crossed. When a boundary is exceeded, the result is a *repercussion*. If a boundary is maintained, the result is a *reward*. When a parent establishes a boundary, the teenager is the one who chooses to go beyond the boundary or to stay within it. This means that the teenager, not the parent, is the one who *chooses the repercussion* or the reward. This also means *the parent no longer wears the black hat!*

One example of a *physical boundary* is the dividing lines drawn for track-and-field events in the Olympic games. In the 100-meter race—the rapid sprint that determines "the fastest man in the world"—all runners burst out of the starting blocks at the sound of the gun. If a runner steps into the lane of another runner in the 100-meter race, the *repercussion* is immediate disqualification. As long as the contestants stay within their boundaries, each runner reaps the *reward* of competing until the end of the race, with the very real possibility of winning the gold.

Anyone involved in sports understands *athletic boundaries.* In football, the ball carrier who stays within the boundary line is given the chance to advance the ball downfield with the hope of scoring. However, the play is called "dead" the instant the ball carrier's foot steps out of bounds. Even if a player *not* carrying the ball steps out of bounds, he cannot continue in the play until the next down. Violators of the boundary line must pay the penalty.

At the Wimbledon Championships, an entire tennis match can hinge on whether the ball lands within the boundary line or a fraction of an inch beyond. In the sports world, boundaries are so important that technicians have perfected the slow-motion instant replay from three different angles to discern if the line is crossed.

In the larger game of life, firmly established boundaries line all areas of life. When you drive a car, you are bound by traffic lanes, stoplights, and speed limits. Ignoring these *motor boundaries* can be fatal. Driving within them can save your life.

Behaviors have boundaries too—*ethical* or *moral boundaries.* Every country has moral boundaries based on its legal system that determine right and wrong. A prime example of both a moral and a legal boundary is theft. From 1932 to 1934, the infamous bank robbers Bonnie and Clyde went on a rampage of crime that included numerous robberies and killings. Ultimately, these notorious outlaws received the *punishment* their *crimes* warranted, both being killed in a massive shootout. Because Bonnie and Clyde crossed both the moral and legal boundaries of the land, they reaped the repercussion of death.

Many young people choose to live outside moral boundaries by engaging in promiscuous sex. To justify themselves, they proclaim, "It's not against the law!" Nevertheless, they still might naturally experience the repercussion of sexually transmitted diseases (STDs), an unwanted pregnancy, or a sexual addiction. What's more, when they cross *biblical boundaries*, they reap the repercussion of God's judgment, disfavor, and lack of blessing. However, teens who remain sexually pure until marriage need not fear STDs. They have the opportunity to enjoy the reward of a clear conscience as well as God's blessing. And someday they can experience the purest relationship possible—pure oneness with their life partner.

What Do You Say to Teens Who Don't Want Boundaries?

Most teenagers want to be free to do what they want to do. Yet imagine a clever young goldfish saying, "I don't like this glass bowl—it's keeping me from going where I want to go—it's too limiting! My goal is to get free of this bowl."

So, one day this young goldfish begins flipping his fins. Soon he learns to jump a little here and leap a little there. Finally, with the flip of his fins and a flap of his tail, he clears the side of the bowl. Now the fish is free! He has met his most challenging goal. He cleared the boundary of the bowl.

But what will happen to our little goldfish? Within a very short time, he will die. This one single act doomed him to certain death. Why?

1. The goldfish needed water.
2. The bowl held the needed water.
3. Therefore, the fish needed the boundary of the bowl to hold the water.

Being free to do whatever you want to do may *seem* right, but that doesn't make it right. As Proverbs 14:12 says, "There is a way that seems right to a man, but in the end it leads to death." This is precisely why young people need their parents' guidance. That's why your teens need you to talk with them about boundaries and explain realistic repercussions and rewards.

What Is the Primary Benefit of Boundaries?

External boundaries are designed to develop *internal* character. When a teenager experiences a negative consequence for defying a boundary, the painful repercussion can be used to develop discipline. Conversely, parents who let their children keep on getting away with wrong are *training* them to do wrong. For example, parents who let a daughter experience no consequences for being disrespectful toward them are training that daughter to be disrespectful toward other authority figures. Consequently, she is learning no self-discipline. Is this in her best interest? Obviously not. A lack of discipline now in her youth does not prepare her for the discipline she will need later in adulthood.

What would typically happen if you had a teenage son who repeatedly reaped no repercussion from coming in after curfew? You would be training him not to respect time. Years later, when he tries to hold down a job, he has no discipline to meet his scheduled deadlines. He has trouble being on time because he was *trained* to disrespect time. This is *not* preparing your kite for flight. This is *not* disentangling your son so that he can soar with self-control.

A short time ago, on a flight from California to Dallas, I sat beside a college freshman. During our conversation I asked, "Did your parents ever give you boundaries and explain repercussions and rewards?"

"*Oh yes,*" he quickly answered.

"Did they enforce them?"

"Oh yes," he replied again with more emotion. "Last year my parents set a midnight curfew for Friday and Saturday nights. Well, one night I let the time slip by, not taking the curfew that seriously. I came in at 2:00, and that was it! My parents refused to let me drive my car for two weeks."

"What impact did that have on you?" I probed.

"It was awful," he moaned. "Every day for the next two weeks, I had to be dependent on somebody driving to my house and taking me to school and someone else driving me home after school. I also had to get rides to and from any activities away from school. I couldn't do anything for myself."

"Did that repercussion make any difference in your life?"

"You bet it did—whenever I was out late, I watched my watch like a hawk!"

"Did you feel your parents were unloving?"

"No, there's no question—they love me. In fact, I know my parents did what they did because they love me," this son spoke with absolute assurance.

"Did you feel that the repercussion was excessive in any way?"

"I thought it was excessive at the time. [But that's what all kids think when a strict consequence is enforced.] Today, I see how the difficulty of being without my car helped me be much more time conscious. Just the fact that I had to pay the consequence for my irresponsibility has helped me be much more responsible. Now that I'm on my own at Texas A & M, I'm thankful for what my parents did—and I think they're great!"

Perhaps the moral of this true story should be summarized in this way: The parent who appears to others to be wearing the black hat will see that, in time, the hat turns white.

CHAPTER 3
QUESTIONS AND ANSWERS ON BOUNDARIES

Fireworks can produce spectacular sights that delight and excite people. Fireworks also can produce dangerous explosives that misfire and maim people. In the context of home and family relationships, if you as a parent establish boundaries for your teens, your entire family could experience explosive "fireworks."

Every successful parent knows that boundaries are essential in order to battle a culture that states: *"There are no moral absolutes."* Even though you have your teenager's best interests at heart, boundaries can ignite caustic attacks from your teen. Verbal assaults can explode all over you and other members of the family. This may cause you to doubt whether you want to maintain boundaries or even set them in the first place.

Questions about boundaries are common among parents, and these questions need to be answered. Sooner or later, these questions could challenge your thinking and cause you to second-guess your previous positive decisions. If you settle the questions now, you need not be mentally attacked with self-doubt when you are in the heat of battle—when you need confidence to stand your ground. The Bible says: "So do not throw away your confidence; it will be richly rewarded. You need to persevere so that when you have done the will of God, you will receive what he has promised" (Heb. 10:35–36).

Is It Really Necessary to Impose Boundaries on Teenagers?

Yes. But as a parent, you are *imparting* boundaries, not *imposing* them. Realize that if your children grow up without boundaries, they will feel frustrated and possibly frightened over the disorder within their lives. In one fascinating sociological study I heard about, researchers took a group of young children and placed them in a large open field to play. There were no fences or boundaries for miles. The researchers then left to watch the children from a hidden location. For the most part, the children huddled close together, playing rather fearfully.

The researchers then took them to a large field bounded by tall, chain-link fencing on all sides and turned them loose. The children wandered all over the field to the far corners of the fencing and played with much greater confidence. Ultimately, the discipline of boundaries will produce a sense of peace in young people, which in turn can bring peace to your soul. The Bible says: "Discipline your son, and he will give you peace; he will bring delight to your soul" (Prov. 29:17).

Won't Boundaries Limit My Teenager's Creativity?

No. Boundaries establish a safe structure that will enhance your teenager's creativity. God created the world with natural boundaries, boundaries such as gravity. Without that boundary, we would not be able to live on the earth He created. Almost everything would be floating in space! In the same vein, He created people with behavioral boundaries—foremost among them the Ten Commandments in Exodus 20—so that we can live in harmony with one another.

Life without these boundaries, where people are free to murder or steal, would be chaotic. Living within moral boundaries, however, provides God's peace, thereby establishing the right breeding ground for creativity in teens. Moral boundaries also help protect your teenager from needlessly stumbling. The Bible says, "Great peace have they who love your law, and nothing can make them stumble" (Ps. 119:165).

Aren't Teenagers Too Old for Parental Discipline?

No. With boundaries you are aiming at a target. Your target is to enable your teenager to become internally motivated to do what is right. In reality, no one outgrows the need for accountability; but teenagers do outgrow certain methods of discipline. Many parents, motivated by love, have spanked their younger children. However, spanking a teenager not only is ineffective, but can also create serious repercussions in the form of alienation.

The purpose of this book is to help you explore methods that are appropriate and practical with teens. In a similar way, the apostle Paul recognized the need for encouraging those closest to him, those who were under his care: "For you know that we dealt with each of you as a father deals with his own children, encouraging, comforting and urging you to live lives worthy of God, who calls you into his kingdom and glory" (1 Thess. 2:11–12).

How Can I Enforce Boundaries without Seeming Cruel?

Make sure your teen knows that you take no pleasure in ruining his day. Take care to comment on the positive character traits you have noticed. Also, remember God's purposes for proper discipline. Boundaries are not just external limits with negative consequences. The goal of a good boundary is to *teach self-control, which in turn develops godly character.* If you do your job as a parent by enforcing discipline at the proper time, your teens may not vote you "The Most Popular Parent of the Year." But wait—all the results are not yet in. The Bible says, "No discipline seems pleasant at the time, but painful. Later on, however, it produces a harvest of righteousness and peace" (Heb. 12:11).

Is There Such a Thing As a Bad Boundary?

Yes. Some boundaries can be too restrictive or too lenient for the age and maturity level of a teen. A parent who insists that a high school student be in at 10:00 on a Friday evening from a school event that isn't even over until 10:00 is being too restrictive. On the other hand, a parent who sets a curfew of midnight on a school night for a high school activity over at 10:00 is being too lenient.

With prayer and observation of your teen, you will be able to discern God's will for each specific situation. However, once you settle on a just boundary, the repercussions as well as the rewards should be made clear and without apology. (Just make sure that the boundary is just.) The Bible gives this warning: "Fathers, do not exasperate your children; instead, bring them up in the training and instruction of the Lord" (Eph. 6:4).

What Are Examples of Appropriate Boundaries?

- A mother tells her chronically late daughter: "We need to be on time for the dinner party, and I know you want to go. If you're ready when the car pulls out at six o'clock, we won't have to go without you." This communication principle is drawn from Proverbs 16:21: "The wise in heart are called discerning, and pleasant words promote instruction."
- A father tells his angry son: "I know you are angry, and I respect your feelings. But if you yell and berate me, your actions only reflect negatively on you. How you express your anger is your choice. I am choosing to leave for a while because what I will allow in my presence is my choice. I hope you will think about a positive way of interacting and that soon we can calmly talk together." This

response is based on Proverbs 29:11: "A fool gives full vent to his anger, but a wise man keeps himself under control."

- A father tells his pouting daughter, who tries to manipulate and control others by her silence: "I always want to talk with you about whatever bothers you, but I will not try to force you to open up. It's clearly your choice when you will be willing to talk. When you are willing, I hope you'll come to me." In this instance, parents are guided by this encouraging proverb: "A wise man's heart guides his mouth and his lips promote instruction" (16:23).

- A mother tells her demanding daughter: "I care about your needs and desires, but I need some time to think about what you are asking. We can talk about it tomorrow." Proverbs 19:2 warns us to think before acting: "It is not good to have zeal without knowledge, nor to be hasty and miss the way."

- A father tells his untrustworthy son: "I know you want me to trust you with the car again, and that's my desire as well. I'm hopeful that we can reestablish trust. For us to work toward that, I need at least a month of your proving that you are trustworthy by going only where you say you are going. Then I can see that you are serious about being trustworthy." Luke 16:10 confirms that someone who is faithful in the little things will be faithful in the big things: "Whoever can be trusted with very little can also be trusted with much, and whoever is dishonest with very little will also be dishonest with much."

More complex, in-depth examples of boundaries are included in the following chapters, most of which have come into our ministry by letter or because of our radio programs. During these broadcasts, we draw from the wisdom of God's Word to address the dilemmas of life. The particular scenarios chosen for this book include real-life illustrations that demonstrate how parents can diffuse the teenage time bombs that often destroy family relationships and how parents can nurture their teenagers to maturity through the use of biblical boundaries.

First and foremost, pray that you will be the wisest parent possible—especially in the midst of "family fireworks." Why not begin each day with this prayer in your heart:

Teach me to do your will,
for you are my God;
may your good Spirit
lead me on level ground.
PSALM 143:10

BOUNDARIES AT SCHOOL

During the academic year, a teenager who is involved in school-sponsored extracurricular activities will spend more waking hours at school than anywhere else, including home. Therefore, problems arising from your teen's behavior will often be apparent at school first. When you are not present to enforce the rules, what do you do when the boundaries are broken? Don't assume that you are powerless as a parent. Even from home, you can set boundaries for school.

CHAPTER 4

TARDINESS

The phone rings. You answer. The vice-principal from your daughter's school informs you that Becky is habitually tardy to class. The reason seems to be that she's using the time between classes to "socialize" in the halls instead of getting to class. Because Becky doesn't have any classes with some of her closest friends, the only time she can talk to them at school is between classes. While you empathize with your daughter's desire to be sociable, Becky's habitual lateness is affecting her grades.

What Can You Do?

- The first and best recourse for parents facing this problem is to get more involved at their school. Get to know your teen's teachers, especially the one whose class time she's missing. Talking to the teacher firsthand (and not taking your teen's word for every situation) cannot only help you understand the situation better, but it will also reassure the teacher that you do care about the situation and you do support her as your teen's teacher.

  A vice-principal at a middle school once told me, "Even if you disagree with some of the teachers' decisions, it's essential for you to maintain an attitude of respect, just as they have to treat parents they disagree with respectfully. If your teenagers hear you criticizing coaches and teachers, they won't have any respect for the school's authority. If you bad-mouth the school at night, it torpedoes those who are in charge of your teen during the day. Then they don't have a chance of getting your kid to cooperate."

- The opposite is also true. A good rule is, "Support in public; confront in private." Be careful not to berate your teen in front of the teacher or anyone else. Too many adults have mental tapes of their parents saying in the presence of others, "You're so lazy! You're so slow! Why can't you do anything right?" Years later, when they are established and successful, those tapes still play over and over again. Therefore, not only confront your teen in private, but also confront school authorities in private without your teen being present—at least initially.

- Once you discern that your teen is indeed guilty of socializing instead of getting to class on time, set appropriate boundaries for the situation. In other words, make sure the punishment fits the crime. Don't overreact. Conversely, don't refuse to act. In the case of tardies, you might choose to add up all the time your daughter has missed from class—perhaps thirty minutes—then double the amount of homework time to an extra sixty minutes. Each minute she's late to class adds another two minutes to homework time.

- Another possibility is for the teen to make up the missed time in study hall. Some schools have policies in place whereby a certain number of tardies automatically draws a detention. Saturday detentions are especially effective.

- Let's assume that your teen experiences the repercussion of crossing the line—goes to detention—but continues to be tardy. In that case, you must elevate the repercussion until you reach a level that evokes a response. Since most teens are social critters, you could ground her from the amount of time she socializes with friends after school or on the phone. Set the restricted time at minutes of class missed, squared (and she gets a free algebra lesson as well)!

- Realize that if you lecture without listening, you will be ineffective. Your daughter must understand that you are on her side. If you set limits without love, you create alienation. Unloving discipline will make her want to get as far away from you as possible: "I can't wait until I'm eighteen and outta here!" Alienating your teen is no way to get her to accept your values. Lead your teenager with love.
- Of course, there may be other, legitimate reasons your teen is continually tardy. In a large high school, it may happen that a student will have third-period class on the south side of the first floor and fourth-period class on the north side of the second floor. Getting from one class to the other within the normal passing period may literally require running, which schools justifiably prohibit. The class period following gym also may be difficult to make on time if the coach does not allow sufficient time for dressing. And, some teachers (being human) have a bad habit of keeping their students after the bell signals the end of class. If any of these scenarios apply, it is even more imperative that you schedule a parent/teacher conference to help straighten out the matter. This is a golden opportunity to be a hero to your teen, which may greatly improve her cooperation with you in other areas.

What Could You Say?

Since we are told to speak the truth in love, how you communicate consequences to an undisciplined teenager is as important as the consequences themselves. You might say, "Becky, I know spending time with your friends is very important to you. And I also want you to be able to spend time with your friends. But it's also important to both of us that you fulfill your responsibilities at school. You need to learn as much as you can in order to prepare for your future. Since it's your responsibility to be on time to your classes and to spend the entire period in class, you owe yourself the schooling you've missed by being late.

"Because you know the school's rules about tardiness, yet still walk in late, you forfeit the right to decide how you're going to spend a certain amount of your free time. You give me no choice but to support the school's discipline. For one week all phone calls to and from friends are suspended Your teachers have been notified to call me if you are tardy If you are not, you can earn back the phone privileges If you are, we'll have to extend the restriction an extra two weeks, which, for your sake, I don't want to do Honey, now it's up to you.

"If you think there's something else we can do to resolve this, I'm willing to listen. We'll do whatever it takes for you to get back in control of your time."

Wisdom from God's Word

Your teenager is not the first teen to be tardy to class. By seeking counsel from school authorities you are being both wise and biblical:

> *Without counsel plans go wrong,*
> *but with many advisers they succeed.*
> PROVERBS 15:22 (RSV)

CHAPTER 5
CUTTING CLASSES

One morning you are at work, up to your ears in deadlines. You receive a call from the secretary at your daughter's school. Bethany's third-period teacher reported her absent. "Is your daughter home sick today?" While the secretary waits for your reply, your heart drops six inches. You know she left for school this morning. You mumble a hasty answer, "Thank you, I'll check into it," and disconnect to call home. The phone rings. The answering machine comes on. She's not at school, and she's not at home. Could she be cutting classes?

When students attain a certain level of confidence at their school, many will try to "beat the system" by cutting classes—that is, being absent from one or more classes without an approved excuse or a note from a parent. The problem is, not only are they missing necessary class instruction, but of greater concern, they are also being deceptive.

If a student is missing from school during the period when overall attendance is taken and the school does not have a note or phone call from the parent, many times the school will call. If the parent is not aware of the teen's absence, the student is declared "truant" for the day, and someone may be sent to look for the student.

Truancy is defined as the unexcused, voluntary absence of a student from school for a set number of days per term. In certain cities, if your teen is truant for ten days or more in any six-month period, both you and your teen will be summoned before a family court judge to explain why. Since you don't want to find yourself in this predicament, you will want to stay on top of the situation. If the school is not efficient about calling you when your teenager skips, the first you may know of it is when you see any number but zero in the "unexcused absences" column of your teen's report card. Once you discover the problem, you must act on it immediately.

What Can You Do?

- Obviously, your first course of action is to talk to the prime suspect—your teenager—as soon as both of you get home. She may have all kinds of excuses, like, "The teacher wasn't paying attention. She never notices me. I was there." Answering this is easy: you call the teacher.
- If the teacher confirms the absences, you may want to do a little probing by asking her these questions:
  — "Do any other students in the class have coincidental absences?"
  — "What are their names?"
  — "Is my daughter having trouble in the class?"
  — "Is she a discipline problem?"
  Although these questions may be difficult to ask, you need to hear whatever the teacher has to say.
- Call the vice-principal, the school counselor, and/or any police officer assigned to full-time duty at the school. Have any of these persons noticed your daughter hanging around with any undesirable students or nonstudents? If she is, they probably would know. Kids do not cut classes to go off alone and "contemplate life." The truant officer will likely know of truant hangouts and what kinds of activities are going on there.

- Even if this incident of skipping school is not a pattern, but only a one time occurrence, find out why she skipped school and with whom. You may find it productive to confront both your daughter and her accomplice. Warn them both that any further unexcused absence will result in notification to the police and termination of their friendship.
- You might also choose to meet with the parents of the accomplice in order to strategize a joint confrontation.

What Could You Say?

Once you have all the information you can get your hands on, then sit down for a heart-to-heart with your daughter. You might say, "Bethany, I have to be honest with you about how hurt I am over this. I view skipping school as very serious for two reasons: you've violated my trust and you've been deceptive.

"You know how much I love you. But now you will no longer have the maneuvering room to deceive me like this. The school has been instructed that, unless I call confirming your legitimate absence, they will call me immediately upon discovering that you are not in class. Then I will alert the police to search for you as a truant, and I will take off work myself to go look for you.

"Moreover, you are grounded from all social activities for the remainder of the six weeks. I know you want me to trust you, and I also want to trust you. But you are the only one who can prove that you will become trustworthy. I love you too much to do nothing. I hope and pray that trust can be restored. That's the desire of my heart."

Wisdom from God's Word

Do not feel guilty about putting limits on your teenager's social activities. The limits you enforce are born out of your love.

Better is open rebuke
than hidden love.
PROVERBS 27:5 (RSV)

CHAPTER 6

DISRUPTING CLASS

You have just learned from your son's teacher that Josh is being disruptive in class by talking, passing notes, and joking around to generate laughter during lecture time. In short, Josh is simply refusing to stay on track. Not only is he failing to learn, but he is also making it very difficult for anyone else to learn. His teacher is growing frustrated and angry, and Josh's grades are beginning to fall.

What Can You Do?

- If you and your teen have not previously established a boundary for this situation, you should sit down with him, communicate what has been shared with you, and ask specifically what happened: "Is it true that you were disruptive in class? What did you do? Who were you trying to make laugh?" Listen carefully, but read between the lines. Only the most saintly teens would not put a little spin on the narrative to reflect more positively on themselves. It may be that your teen will level with you. If he takes ownership of the undesirable behavior and admits what he did wrong, then discuss his options. Explain that if it happens again, the only thing that you know to do is join him in class. This way, you're giving him fair warning and the opportunity to correct the problem himself.

- If your son continues to be the class clown, the most memorable solution, because it is the most dreaded, is to rearrange your schedule and join your teen in the classroom that he is disrupting (of course request permission from the teacher first). You could either sit at the back of the room, or—for greater effect—sit right next to your son. Just the thought of having "Mommy" or "Daddy" sit by him while his peers look on can make the rowdiest teen sober.

- Should your schedules not allow you to join your teen in school, you might find another respected adult relative to sit in for you.

- Or you may choose to set another repercussion such as cutting back on the time your son socializes with the other teens he is trying to impress.

What Could You Say?

You might say, "Josh, I appreciate how entertaining you are. Your natural humor makes me laugh. And I know how fun it is to make the other kids laugh. But we need to appreciate how frustrated the teacher feels trying to compete with you for the class's attention. Remember how upset you got when your sister started talking over you at dinner? Well, the teacher has a certain amount of material she's required to cover each day, and when you're talking, she can't do that.

"You're mature enough to know when it's OK to joke around with your friends and when it's not. I know that you know what appropriate classroom behavior is. And I believe you have the self-control needed—you're just not exercising it. Because you can exercise self-control around me, it seems that you need my presence to remind you to be quiet and pay attention."

If your son maintains that the teacher has an unwarranted grudge against him, you could counter: "It may be that the teacher is all wrong and you're right when you say you're not doing anything disruptive. But there's got to be some reason she keeps being concerned about your behavior. The only way for me to find out what's really going on is to sit in on your class. When we both decide you don't need me there anymore, I'll leave. I have every confidence that with the right motivation, you can exercise self-control in any situation, and I'm going to do whatever's necessary to help you get there, even if it's inconvenient for me and embarrassing to you."

Wisdom from God's Word

By helping your son check his disruptive chatter and tame his tongue, you enable him to have more self-control and even to apply a biblical standard. Since the Bible says certain actions are to be avoided, hand him this Scripture on an index card and encourage him to memorize it:

Avoid godless chatter, because those who
indulge in it will become more and more ungodly.
2 TIMOTHY 2:16

CHAPTER 7
FAILING GRADES

Your daughter Diane began the school year with optimism. But as her enthusiasm drained and her grades sank, you have found yourself floating on a sea of dismay. Time and again, you've reminded her to do her homework, but to no avail. To this day you see no improvement. You feel distraught. You don't even know what the problem is. And unless the real problem gets corrected, Diane has no option but to fail.

What Can You Do?

- At this point, a parent/teacher conference is paramount. You and your teen's teacher should probe for the real reason the homework is not being done. Is your daughter overcommitted to too many activities? If so, something may have to go. Does she not understand the material? If so, tutoring may help. Or, as is usually the case, is the homework just not a priority? If so, the teacher can help you set up an accountability system to help motivate your daughter to complete the work. Solicit feedback from the teacher about your teen's behavior during class, without becoming defensive.

- Talk with your teen to find out what the problem is from her perspective. Suggest that she come up with a solution, and then discuss it with her. Kids can be quite creative. In fact, they can surprise you when you challenge them to think. This may work—it may not. The bottom line is that your teen needs to learn how to manage time well and prioritize what is important each day. Obviously, you need to tie privileges to getting homework done, such as no TV or telephone calls over three minutes before homework assignments are completed *to your satisfaction.*

- You might designate a specific time for doing homework each day and make her stick to that—no phone calls, no visits, no interruptions of any kind. You may need to take on the role of homework monitor for a while. Find out what kind of assignments are involved, when tests are coming up, and what needs to be studied. Then help your daughter pace herself. Dredge your memory for the motivators that helped you get your schoolwork done.

- If the weight of your teenager's study habits is falling wholly on your shoulders, look at the academic strengths and weaknesses of your teen. For instance, in ninth grade, I loved algebra and made straight A's. Because I love puzzles, I liked algebra. Figuring out the equations was like putting a puzzle together. What helped me most though was that we had homework to turn in every day. The math teacher provided my daily impetus for working on and learning the material. However, in other subjects like history, where we were not given daily assignments, I had greater difficulty, especially if we only had a few tests covering many chapters. I had a harder time pacing myself— and still do—with tasks that required long-range planning.

- You could help by breaking large assignments or tests down into small, bite-size chunks. (As the old saying goes: "How do you eat an elephant? One bite at a time!") Discovering your teen's learning style will provide a clue as to what kind of help is needed.

- There is another common and extremely distressing reason for failure, especially among bright or gifted students:

burnout. Because of our desire to enable gifted students to achieve their full potential, parents, teachers, and administrators start looking at very young students, even preschoolers, for indications of giftedness. Those so earmarked go into special honors or accelerated programs in which they are expected to master more difficult subject matter than their other classmates. Each year the pressure to achieve is increased, culminating in very competitive high school programs designed to garner scholarships into even more competitive universities.

Tragically, the higher suicide rate of high achieving students indicates just how intolerable the stress can get. One boy began elementary school in the gifted program, yet by the time he was a senior in high school, he was struggling just to pass enough regular classes to graduate on time. He was burned out.

Any budding athlete, dancer, musician, thespian, linguist, scientist, mathematician (and the list goes on) can suffer a similar fate at the hands of adults anxious to capitalize on the teen's abilities. Parents would do well to be wary of too many programs, too many competitions, too much pushing. Watch your teen for signs of stress: difficulty sleeping, unhealthy eating, peevishness, or constant anxiety. If you see these signs, reevaluate your teen's activities at once.

Offer him the option to quit, then watch his reaction. Even scaling back can help. One Dallas mother made this candid comment: "My daughter has always excelled in English. So I was floored when she told me she wanted to drop out of honors English and take regular English instead during her junior year. I opened my mouth to absolutely forbid it, and the Lord reminded me, 'You dropped out of honors algebra in your junior year of high school.' I had indeed, and it saved my sanity. So I told her she could. It turned out to be the right thing to do."

• Sometimes teens struggle with their grades because they are experiencing some pain in their lives, some heartache of which you're not even aware. I remember the tenth grade as being the worst year of my life. That was the year I chose to confront my father about his infidelity. Because of that, I was sent off to boarding school. One quarter that year I failed all my classes except one; in that one I got a D. I wasn't focused on school. I wasn't focused on friends. My focus was on protecting my mother, and my heart was in the deepest despair.

During that time, I remember appreciating the fact that my mom didn't scold me about my grades. But I knew she cared about my heart. And since she didn't know what to do about our home situation either, we just struggled along. Fortunately, along the way I became an authentic Christian and that *changed life* changed my heart and changed my perspective.

For a few months that year I had a tutor—a wonderful, non-judgmental woman who made me feel that I was valued and that somehow I'd make it through. I never shared personal details of my life with her, but I felt that I could confide in her if I wanted to because I knew she cared about me. Just her caring heart helped beyond measure.

What Could You Say?

If your teenager has failing grades, motivation is a must. Just realize that if your teenager is motivated with hope, she can learn almost anything. Years ago, I learned a study tactic that I have shared with many students. In fact, one day not long ago, I met a high school student thoroughly discouraged about how poorly she was doing in math. "You're having trouble understanding the math principles—is that it?" I asked. When she confirmed my assumption, I said, "I know something that can make a huge difference. But would you be willing to devote a weekend beginning Saturday morning to tackle math?"

"Anything," Kris replied desperately. "I cannot flunk this class." "Then start back at the beginning of the book. Read every word on every page at the beginning, where the book explains the foundational concepts. It will be quite easy for a number of chapters because you have been doing algebra problems for months. At the end of each chapter, there is always a test. You'll love it because those tests will be a snap. But make sure to work each problem so that you can understand the principle. Work your way through the book, exercise by exer-

cise. You will actually have fun understanding algebra." With only the tiniest mustard seed of hope, she promised to try.

Several months later I got a letter from Kris, telling me ecstatically that she had brought her grade up from a D to an A! All along she had thought she was stupid at math, that she would always struggle in math and not understand the principles behind the problems. But this simple study method of going back to the beginning of the book enabled her to capture the concepts she had missed.

I learned this study method by watching my college roommate. Both of us were taking Italian. She had an A an average. My grade had slipped to a C+ going into the final exam. When I saw Linda go back to the beginning of the book and do the language exercises page by page, I did the same. To my amazement, I made a 98 on the final exam and earned an A for the semester. The teacher even commented about how impressed she was that I performed so well on the final. The credit went to my roommate. I only wish I had known that study method years before.

If you have a teenager struggling to "make the grade," emphasize: "For the remainder of this six weeks, your social activities on school nights, including talking on the phone, are suspended. Every night you are to spend a minimum of two hours studying, then review with me what you've done before getting ready for bed. Once you have improved your grades, you can gradually resume your social activities so long as your grades remain up. You are not stupid. You just need to study in a way that is smart. It's going to take effort, but with God's help, you can do it."

Wisdom from God's Word

Take the pressure off your teen by explaining that she doesn't need to work to please you. Instead, if she'll just do her best, she is pleasing God.

Whatever you do, work at it with all your heart,
as working for the Lord, not for men.
COLOSSIANS 3:23

CHAPTER 8
CHEATING

Late one afternoon while your son is gone, one of his friends calls to ask for the page number of that night's homework assignment in history. Trying to be helpful, you open your son's binder to locate the assignment. There, you discover a homework paper clearly not his. First you feel perplexed. Then your heart sinks in dismay as you study the paper. Did Chris really copy someone else's homework? Has he been cheating? Does he consistently cheat without your knowing about it?

■

A recent newspaper survey found that a far larger percentage of today's high school and college students cheat on their schoolwork than ever before in the history of the poll. The reasons may be due not just to the decreasing moral standards of the last few decades, but also to the increasing costs of college (thus, the competition for scholarships) and the increasing availability of "tools" that facilitate cheating. For example, on the Internet, certain web sites offer term papers on a wide variety of topics, available to download for a fee, of course. Interestingly, the students who most frequently cheat are not the ones most in danger of failing, but the ones who already make high grades. They cheat to maintain the highest GPA (grade point average) possible with the hope of graduating with top honors. However, dishonest grades only reap dishonor.

What Can You Do?

• Initially discern if your son is actually cheating. What one teacher may consider cheating, another may encourage, such as "cooperative homework." If you observe homework being shared, you might say, "Do you think you are learning that material well enough for a test?" Your son's reaction of:

— confidence ("Oh, sure, no problem.")

— embarrassment ("Uh, I hope so.")

— defensiveness ("I will, I already, so leave me alone!")

could be an indication of whether or not he's cutting corners with the homework. If he is, the best "teacher" may be to let him learn by taking his lumps at test time. Then the natural consequences for his negative behavior will kick in . . . unless, of course, he then cheats on the test.

• Although you can't be casing out the classroom, most teachers who catch students cheating give them automatic zeros. So an obvious clue would be to notice any unexplained zeros on your son's progress reports.

• Another option is to quiz your teenager the evening before the next several tests in order to evaluate his knowledge of the material. If he is consistently ill-prepared, consider reviewing his homework on a daily basis. One mother confided, "Chris does not test well. Even if he knows the material, he gets so uptight during tests that he feels compelled to glance at other papers nearby. When his seventh-grade teacher noticed him doing this, she just turned his chair around to face the wall. He came home embarrassed enough to decide he was going to change, somehow. Before his next test, I sat down and went over and over the material with him until he knew it backward and forward. As a result, he wasn't so tempted to peek."

- Regarding his class participation, speaking with his teachers may prove to be helpful. You can also request suggestions on how to help your son at home. After consulting with the teacher, consider all your options. One of the best ways to help your teen overcome a dependence on plagiarism is to be your teen's accountability partner. Keep yourself informed regarding all reports your teen will need to do during a grading period or during a semester. Help your teen establish and follow through on a reading schedule. This will prepare him for his written reports. Additionally, you could:

— Engage him in conversation regarding what he is reading.

— Review with him the class notes or textbook.

— Give him a quiz over the material.

— Have him read his paper to you or give you a copy to read yourself before turning it in at school.

Make it clear to your teen that his job is that of being a student and that both you and the Lord want him to be the best student he can possibly be. Challenge your teen to learn all that he can. Encourage him to maintain his integrity in the classroom so that he will have a clear conscience and be a witness to his classmates. Explain that cheating is the equivalent of stealing. And spiritually, cheating will hinder his prayers and block the favor of God on his life. Psalm 6:12 says, "For surely, O Lord, you bless the righteous. You surround them with your favor as with a shield."

What Could You Say?

If cheating is a part of your teen's life, address it head-on and establish clear consequences. You might say something like this:

"Son, you know I love you and always want the best for you. While cheating on homework or on a test may seem insignificant to you, cheating is very significant to God, as well as to me. I realize that your goal is to get a good grade, and that's an appropriate goal. But on God's test of integrity,

you can't get a passing grade if you cheat on tests at school. Your grades count for this present time, but your integrity counts for eternity.

"God is far more concerned that you have Christlike character than great grades. My responsibility as a parent is to see that you have the same priority. So for now, all of your social privileges are suspended until you settle this matter of integrity for yourself and then decide how you'll demonstrate to me that it is settled. In the deepest part of your heart, I know you want to live a life of integrity. I'm more than willing to help you any way that I can." Then talk through a possible plan.

Wisdom from God's Word

Give your teenager this proverb which, in regard to cheating, presents both a reward and a repercussion. Then ask him to read it each night just before turning off the light.

The integrity of the upright guides them,
but the unfaithful are destroyed by their duplicity.
PROVERBS 11:3

CHAPTER 9
FIGHTING

What a shock to get a phone call from your son's principal. He matter-of-factly informs you that Rick has been in a fight at school and bloodied the nose of another student. Moreover, you find out that Rick initiated the fight by throwing the first punch. The school nurse treated the other boy at the scene, and the school resource officer filed a police report. As a result of this fracas, you have to pick up your son immediately. He is suspended from school until you can meet with the principal in a conference. At this time, the principal doesn't know whether the parents of the other boy intend to press charges or bring a lawsuit.

What Can You Do?
- Your best response is immediate action. Set up the school conference as soon as possible. Cooperate with the officials in setting the repercussion. Although you will talk to your son about what happened, and may even feel a certain sympathy for him, this is not the time to come to his rescue. You must allow the experience to teach him that striking out in anger hurts himself more than anyone.

Fights rarely happen out of the blue. Most likely, a precipitating situation has been simmering for some time. For example, the other boy could have been provoking your son with continual taunts or teasing, shoving, or profanity. As you discuss the situation with the school representatives, keep an open mind to their appraisal of the situation, including their recommendations for resolution. Above all, your teen must hear you say, "We take full responsibility for this." If it makes him angry to hear this because he doesn't feel responsible, privately explain how his attempt to resolve the matter with violence has damaged your ability to defend him.

- The first goal here is for your son to accept personal responsibility for what *he* did, regardless of other factors. He had other choices that he simply did not exercise. Most often, he will not seriously consider any of these choices in the future unless he experiences a painful repercussion.
- If you are permitted, having a face-to-face meeting with the other boy and his parents is most desirable. Your son must start off with a sincere apology, including an offer to pay medical expenses. For most people, a penitent attitude goes a long way toward ameliorating the legal ramifications. They probably do not really want to drag you to court or see your son in jail. They want an apology for the assault and an assurance that it won't happen again. The apology also greatly helps in clearing the air between the two combatants. When the adults demonstrate this kind of peacemaking, more than likely the teens will follow suit.

  Many a teenager has been "thrown into the tank" (for the uninitiated, that's not a swimming pool, but a jail cell). And, as a result, a loving parent will choose not to bail him out immediately, realizing that a painful ordeal can provide a powerful turnaround in the life of a troubled teen.
- Your son must complete, with a reasonably good attitude, whatever disciplinary or probationary exercises that follow, such as community service. If your attitude is that this repercussion is a must, he most likely will do the work. (And if you are right there with him mowing yards, he might surprise you with his overt willingness to do it.)

Because you are in no way going to reward him for losing his temper, all social functions should be suspended at once. Now, with all his free time at home, ask him to write down all the options he could have chosen when he felt angry. Meanwhile, make your own list. Then, at a regular time each week, get together and talk about any feelings of anger and about his positive options. Use this time to build a relationship with him.

- If the fight resulted from gang activity, you have another problem altogether. Gangs are no longer confined to inner cities, but have been spreading into suburbia like wildfire. The sense of belonging, of empowerment, of secrecy, and of living on the edge tends to make kids who feel disenfranchised vulnerable to the lure of gang membership. That's why boys from two-parent, middle-class homes often dress like rap stars and talk with ghetto slang. In a recent highly publicized case, a boy at a predominantly white, upper-middle-class high school gouged out another boy's eyes in a gang fight, blinding him for life. Since both were juveniles, the parents of the aggressor agreed to send him to military school across the country as both a repercussion and rehabilitation.

- Don't assume that your teen could never be drawn into gang activity. If you notice your son spending a lot of time away from home with undesirable friends, or continually wearing certain clothing and unfamiliar emblems, or assuming a different dialect, stance, or gestures, be forewarned. It's time for you to start playing Sherlock Holmes to discover his level of involvement.

Talk to him, but don't be surprised if he won't respond—loyalty is a primary attribute of gang membership. You will need help from your school resource officer or your police department's gang unit to find out what gang you're dealing with, how dangerous they are, and who the rival gangs are.

You must take measures to reintegrate your son into your family and to make him understand his worth and unique role as a family member. Grounding a young

man already involved in gang activities may be futile—either you will have to move, or he will have to come to the decision himself that this lifestyle is not for him. It may be helpful to attend sessions with a gang counselor who can show your son morgue photos of the casualties of gang warfare. Above all, remember the power of spiritual warfare. Pray diligently and look for the Lord's deliverance.

What Could You Say?

You might tell him, "Look, son, I'm standing by you, no matter what. I know you had a legitimate complaint about this boy. You had a right to be upset. If you had gone to the coach or any high school official or even to me about your problem with him, we could have done something to help you. But losing control as you did just makes you come across as the bad guy. Now people see you as a bigger problem than he is! You know there's someone at my office who cuts me down all the time. What do you think would happen if I handled this like you did? I'd be arrested, spend time in jail, lose my job, and couldn't provide for the family.

"We all feel anger at times. Being angry is not the problem. How you expressed your anger is the problem. Your anger was out of control. No matter what someone does to provoke you, you need to be in control of *you*. Does it feel good for you to be out of control? (He'll probably say *no*.)

"One of the basic tenets in the martial arts describes the relationship between self-respect and self-control: *He cannot respect himself if he cannot control himself.*

"I'm committed to helping you grow in the areas of self-respect and self-control. Right now, because you are having difficulty displaying self-control and are a harm to others, you leave me no choice but to restrict the time after school and on weekends that you can be with others. All social functions are suspended until I feel confident that you can control yourself. I am committed to helping you learn the value of acting responsibly toward people, and I'll do whatever it takes to help you do that."

Wisdom from God's Word

Fighting and all other forms of violence erupt out of unresolved anger. Help your son see that God calls out-of-control anger "sin"—an anger over which he can have control.

In your anger do not sin;
when you are on your beds,
search your hearts and be silent.
PSALM 4:4

CHAPTER 10
SEXUAL HARASSMENT

Your normally outgoing daughter has suddenly became anxious and withdrawn. She's reluctant to go to school and reluctant to talk about what is bothering her. Mary's fearful behavior is quite unlike her. When you finally confront her and press for an explanation, she ashamedly admits that Jason has been sexually harassing her at school.

What Can You Do?
For a Daughter Who Is Being Harassed:

- Your first challenge in helping your daughter is simply to find out exactly what happened. Getting her to talk with you about something so intimately painful builds a healthy relationship. Treat what she says very seriously, and encourage her to be specific:
  - Who was involved?
  - What was said?
  - What was done?
  - How did she respond?
  - Where did it happen?
  - What were the circumstances?

— How often has it happened?

— Did anyone else see or hear it happen?

— If so, who?

— Whom has she told?

— What are her fears?

— What is she feeling about the harasser?

— How is she feeling about herself?

Take notes on everything she says.

- Emphasize that due to the seriousness of the situation, you must take her to report the misconduct to the school administrators, who are legally required to investigate any such reports in a fair, exhaustive manner. Prepare her by saying that they will grill her like a chicken sandwich, especially if the accusation is about a faculty or staff member. Any inconsistencies or apparent falsehoods will cast severe doubts on her credibility. Warn her not to make up "something" just to fill in what she can't remember. Once you get the authorities involved, there's no turning back. Therefore, you and she must be sure of her facts.

- It may be that some harassment is going on, but your daughter does not want to make an official complaint. Girls from Christian families are generally brought up to be polite, cooperative, and trusting, and many are totally unprepared to deal with un-Christian behavior from others. But the world is a battle zone in which both male and female Christians are required to display courage, intelligence, and resourcefulness. If your daughter has to run to the authorities for protection against the bad boys in the hall who make obscene suggestions, how is she ever going to stand against the onslaughts of the world? For this reason, it may actually be preferable that she handle it herself. You may need to equip her to face this test herself. One caveat: if the offender is an adult, you *must* inform the authorities, even if your daughter does not want to. She cannot be expected to handle such a situation herself. It's not a fair fight.

- If you and your daughter have determined to face this war on your own, start with an in-depth personality analysis— of her. There are two types of girls who tend to draw the most sexual harassment: girls who look like they want it, and girls who look like they are afraid of it (those who look vulnerable or helpless).

- The two of you could evaluate the way she dresses for school:
    — Is her dress even slightly provocative?
    — Is she wearing too much makeup?
    — Is she wearing too much jewelry?

If so, then she's sending signals and not realizing it. Without accusing or blaming, you need to make certain she sees how she could be contributing to the problem of being a target sexually. A young woman who tries to dress like a sex symbol or pop star should not take offense when men respond sexually. While inappropriate dress does not excuse inappropriate actions on the part of men, your daughter must take responsibility for the image she projects.

- Likewise, the two of you should evaluate if your daughter is viewed as weak or vulnerable:
    — Is she extremely shy and timid, walking with her head down, books clutched to her chest?
    — Does she hesitate to speak up in class even though she knows the answers?
    — Is she constantly apologizing for things that are not her fault?

If these apply, then in the twisted thinking of many immature male teens, she's begging for harassment. Let her know that abusers look for those whom they can successfully abuse. Help her walk and talk confidently. Coach her in walking with her head up (without making eye contact with harassers), shoulders back, and strong strides. Show her how to carry her books in a less defensive manner. Teach her to respond to verbal attacks with a silent but steady glare. She need not undergo a personality change; she needs to develop backbone. In any case, you both should remember to pray for the person whose life is so empty that he (the harasser) feels the need to relate to others in this way.

For a Son Who Is Harassing a Girl:

- If it is your son doing the harassing, you may not know anything about it until you are contacted by his school. Then, after you have picked yourself up off the floor, talk with him to find out *exactly* what is going on. Ask the five Ws: Who, Where, What, When, and Why?

- Some boys do not know how to approach a girl without harassing or stalking her. If grown men have trouble ascertaining the level of a female's interest—and some do—it's going to be that much harder for a teenager. In fact, her interest is the crucial factor: if she's interested, he's flirting; if she's not interested, he's harassing. Compounding this difficulty is the fact that the girl does not have to tell the boy that he is offending her for his behavior to be considered harassment. All she has to do is tell someone else.

- If the harassment was unintentional, and your son is remorseful and/or embarrassed by the girl's reaction, then tutor him in how to read subtle, conflicting female signals. If a girl makes a complaint, he must absolutely leave her alone. He must not talk to her, look at her, or talk *about* her to other people at school. If he does, it can be considered retaliation and will get him into even greater trouble.

  In the future, if he is interested in a girl, suggest that he visualize himself driving down a street through a series of intersections for which *she* controls the stoplights. If he comes to a red light, he must stop. He cannot proceed. If he gets a green light, he can proceed, but only to the next intersection—he cannot continue to barrel through every intersection.

  The first traffic light is eye contact and facial expression. When he is around her, or speaks to her, does she make eye contact with him? Does she smile at him? If she does neither, that is a red light. He may attempt to converse with her about school matters, but he must not try to go beyond that.

  If she does make eye contact and smile, that does not mean she is in love with him. She could simply be a naturally friendly person. But he nonetheless has a green light to the next intersection, which is proximity and general attitude:

— If he attempts to stand close enough to her to whisper (for example), does she let him stay there, or does she back away?

— Does she linger to talk to him, or does she turn her back on him to talk to someone else?

— Does she initiate conversation with him?

— Does she give him notes (meant for him and not someone else)?

— Does she touch him?

All these are green lights. He can proceed down the street.

(At this point, with increasing closeness and touching, you as a parent could get queasy, wondering what is coming up at the next intersection.) In no uncertain terms, he should stay on this stretch for a long time. Part of your job as a parent is to make sure that the intersections do not lead to more personal territory (see chap. 37, "Sexual Activity"). He also should be reminded that lights can change from green to red, and he must stop when they do. If he is mature enough, he can ask her what went wrong, but he should know that persistence in trying to resolve matters can lead to charges of harassment. However, if he has been watchful at the intersections, she will have sent a caution sign as a warning.

- If you discover that your son has been harassing a girl for the sake of harassment, *then* you can lower the boom on him because this is indefensible. Lecture all you want about respect for others and how his behavior reflects on you, but be aware of the other factors at work, specifically, his friends. This kind of behavior usually happens for the benefit of an "audience." So when you are questioning him, be sure to ask who else heard it and who else participated. If you hear the same name(s) cropping up again and again when your son has been in trouble, then you know you're contending with a group problem. You may try to break up the pack by:

— contacting the parents of his cohorts and gaining their perspectives and cooperation in stopping the harassment

— grounding your son from spending free time with other troublemakers

— asking his teachers to separate them in class

— asking the principal to separate them at lunch and other activities

— steering your son toward other friends, a positive church youth group, a fascinating hobby . . . or even a job

These measures may not work because the social caste system at school can be ironclad. But at least you are not giving him a green light to head down the road of harassment unheeded.

What Could You Say?

To Your Son:

Initially your son may fiercely resent your intrusion into his social life. But you need to be up front with him. "Jason, believe me, I am for you no matter what difficulty you're in. I know this is a tough time. And that's why we have to talk. Under no circumstances are you to touch Mary in any way. You are not even to talk or walk with her. Don't joke with her or about her. Keep your mouth shut about Mary. If someone asks you about what happened, you will be respected if you simply say, "It was my fault. I acted inappropriately. But I won't do it again." Ask Jason to repeat each sentence with you.

"Son, you also need to say those words to Mary and ask her to forgive you. I will try to set up a time for you to call her or meet with you briefly. I will be right by your side. The Bible says, 'He who conceals his sins does not prosper, but whoever confesses and renounces them finds mercy'" (Prov. 28:13 RSV).

"I don't want to have to curtail your free time with others, but once you crossed a sexual boundary, you've left me no choice. For a month, no outside activities after school or on weekends.

"I want to be able to trust you again. If you prove yourself trustworthy, your privileges will be restored. I believe you can be trustworthy. Son, don't let me or yourself down. I have no desire to ruin your life. But accusations of sexual harassment can ruin your life."

To Your Daughter:

Being sexually harassed is at the same time both angering and demeaning. Your daughter really needs your help in acknowledging her feelings as well with how to respond appropriately to the harassment. "Honey, I know that you are in no way to blame. What's happened to you is so wrong. If at times you wonder 'What did I do to cause this?' just know that you did nothing. No one makes another person behave inappropriately.

"It hurts me that someone would say such degrading things to you. At times you may feel like crawling into a hole. At the same time you may feel anger. When you do, just know that you're experiencing justifiable anger. The Bible says, 'Be angry, but do not sin.' You can feel anger, but then you need to release it so that you will not be consumed by it. Never feel it's wrong to report sexual harassment. You are on the side of truth, and truth will set you free. Let's pray together for a couple of days about how the Lord wants you to see this situation and how He wants you to handle it. Then we'll talk again and see what the Lord has revealed to each of us. And let's pray for Jason too. He really needs the Lord in his life."

Wisdom from God's Word

No matter what you and your daughter decide to do about the sexual harassment, most important is the attitude of her heart. While it is human nature to respond with anger, it is the Lord's nature to respond in love. By praying for the unmet need in this young man's life, she is not acting weak; she is doing something strong.

Do not be overcome by evil,
but overcome evil with good.
ROMANS 12:21

One of the most graphic Scriptures on sexual sin is found in the Book of Proverbs. After giving it to your son, pray that it will continue to burn in his heart:

Can a man scoop fire in his lap
without his clothes being burned?
PROVERBS 6:27

SECTION 3
BOUNDARIES AT HOME

We all want "home" to be a place of peace—a refuge
from the wrongs of the world—for everyone in the family.
But if a teenager resides at home, it can become a
battleground over rights and responsibilities. In order to
have "home sweet home," boundaries are essential . . . not
just for your teen's sake, but also for the sake of everyone
else who must share the living space.

CHAPTER 11
SHIRKING CHORES

"Kerry—come in here! You were supposed to clean off the table. No, you can't wait till after the TV show!" You feel anxious because the Mortons are arriving for dinner in less than 30 minutes.

"Julie, I asked you to pick up everything off the floor an hour ago! What have you been doing?" Although you're trying to talk to your teenagers, you feel like you're talking to the air.

"Tom! Your deadline for getting the yard work done was yesterday. Absolutely nothing has been done!" You know your teenagers have been shirking their responsibilities. This is nothing new.

What Can You Do?

- First, understand that you are not doing your teenagers a favor by allowing them to get by without helping at home. Whenever they leave your home, whether it's to live with roommates or a marriage partner, the idea that they are too "special" to do menial work will not make for a happy home in their new living quarters. For example, if your daughter cannot understand the obligation she has to her housemates to clean up after herself, she won't have housemates for long. Then she'll have to come back home . . . just when you were used to seeing everything neat and orderly. One important point to emphasize to your daughter is that being faithful to do her chores is a way to show respect for those who are closest to her.

- Early on, when America was an agricultural society, it was commonly understood that children would have significant chores around the house or farm. But with the lifestyle of the twenty-first century, many teenagers consider themselves too important to have household chores. (I saw a poster the other day that seemed to express the mood of the day: "Teenagers: Tired of being hassled by your parents? Act now! Move out while you still know everything.") The inescapable fact is: *everyone* in the home should share in the responsibilities that keep a household running smoothly. All who live at home have general responsibilities that include taking care of personal bedrooms by making beds and picking up items from the floor. The individual responsibilities are daily or weekly assignments, such as taking out the trash, cleaning the kitchen, mowing the lawn, vacuuming, sweeping the sidewalk and doing the laundry. Some teenagers know exactly which chores are theirs, but they don't do them without constant reminders.

- Once you decide on a fair allocation of chores, explain your rationale to your teenagers during a "family council meeting." Have them repeat to you what they've heard and present any scheduling problems. After the problems are ironed out, everyone agrees, and that's it! Post the schedule. No grumbling allowed. Otherwise, it becomes a never-ending argument: "Why do I have to do the dishes? I did them last night." "Why do I have to clean the windows? They're not dirty." "Why do I have to cut the grass? It's not that high." If you have established who should complete each chore and by when—in writing—then you can hold your ground without resorting to the old parental groaner, "Because I said so." You can do this because increased responsibility results in increased freedom. This means you hold the trump card: your daughter's personal freedom depends on whether she has done her assigned chores *to your satisfaction.* That is, she will not leave to pass the time with her friends until her room passes inspection!

• One mother offered this insight: "My favorite phrase for dealing with messy rooms (or poor grades, or a bad attitude) is: 'That's not like you.' It's a truism that children actually live up, or down, to our expectations of them. If I see that Jennifer's room is trashed—again—and say, 'You are such a slob!' that just reinforces her notion that she can't keep her room clean. She won't even try.

"The first time I used this tactic with Jennifer about her room, I remarked, 'This clutter isn't like you. You're usually so well organized.' She rolled her eyes and looked at me as if I were a bold-faced liar. She even said, 'You're crazy! I'm not organized!' I said, 'Maybe you haven't acted that way recently, but you're really an organized person on the inside.'

"Seeing results from this has taken time because I had to change the way I speak to her, and she had to change her perception of herself. But it's paying off."

• Now, about the laundry: Don't let the dirty clothes of teens give you the "wash day blues." Draw the "clothesline" and stay behind it. Laundry that does not make it to the hamper does not get washed. If Kent really wants his favorite red shirt for Friday, he will somehow find the strength to move it ten feet from the floor to the hamper, but in no way will the dedicated laundry person be forced to search out his dirty clothes.

• Do not take responsibility for making sure your teenagers do their chores. They may pretend not to understand, but you have already discussed these and have put them in writing. They may "forget," but you must choose not to nag. If you give your teenagers the same instructions over and over again, then you are teaching them that they don't have to obey until you've said it the fourth, fifth, or sixth time. You must discipline yourself to enforce the consequences if the chores aren't done. This is the harder task because your teen will come up with the most heartrending excuses imaginable.

What Could You Say?

Let's say your son should have mowed the lawn by 6 P.M. Saturday. It's now 6:45 P.M. and he's heading out the door. He says, "I promise I'll do it tomorrow. I give you my word. Susie finally agreed to go out with me, and I'll look like a total dork if I tell her I can't go because I have to mow the lawn. Please, don't do this to me. Please! She'll never speak to me again."

With calm, sober sympathy, stretch out your hand for his car keys. "I'm so sorry, Kent. I want you to be able to go out with Susie, but it was your choice to sleep late this morning and watch sports this afternoon instead of mowing the lawn. You've known all week that you couldn't go anywhere today until that was done. Susie will forgive you." If he misses his date, he will learn:

— you mean what you say;
— his obligation to keep his word to his parents takes precedence over his obligations to his friends;
— he cannot alter agreements with you when it suits him;
— you are still in charge.

And I would venture to say that next week Kent will do his chores on time so that he can enjoy the privilege of taking Susie out . . . and yes, Susie will still be speaking to him.

Wisdom from God's Word

Since most teenagers are known for having bottomless pits when it comes to food, perhaps this Scripture will have a motivating impact.

"If a man will not work, he shall not eat."
2 THESSALONIANS 3:10

CHAPTER 12
MONEY TROUBLES

Your son has developed a hole in his pocket or an unquench-able appetite for something. Within a week he has managed to spend his entire monthly allowance. When you approach him about it, he unloads on you, "Dad, if I show up at school in something uncool, I'll get laughed off campus!" The last thing you want is for Kurt to be laughed at or rejected!

"And how can I invite anybody over if I don't have the lat-est CDs? Nobody'd come! And everybody meets at Chuckie's after school for burgers—am I supposed to say, 'Sorry, can't afford it'? And how am I going to get to know Stephanie if I can't take her out anywhere? Come on, Dad!"

Sound familiar? You feel pressure building up inside your heart. You're thinking, *Kurt, you don't know half of what it costs to raise a teenager!* You well know the expenses of a teen who is driving: gas, car insurance, maintenance, repairs. Of course, there are the school-related expenses: band uniforms, trips, project supplies, club dues, fund-raisers. Then there are church youth group expenses: retreats, conferences, choir mission trips. Moreover, the least of these expenses is not computer equipment, which is rapidly becoming the norm for doing school work or preparing to earn a living. Meanwhile, as you're trying to tuck away money for college, he complains that he is a social outcast for his lack of cash. Not only are you hard-pressed to help, but you also don't agree with everything he feels he needs.

What Can You Do?

- One obvious solution may be a part-time job. Many teens work—out of sheer necessity. In Texas, teens as young as fourteen can work limited hours in specified fields, such as retail and food service. The problems come when employers start expecting more hours than a full-time student can comfortably work, or when your teen's grades start suffering. Also, sports, volunteer work, or extracurricular activities, all of which are important to college admissions offices, sometimes preempt the possibility of a part-time job during the week.

- Many businesses have such a dire need of regular, reliable help, that with a little effort, your teen might be able to locate an employer who will accommodate whatever hours he can work, even if it's only on Saturdays. You should insist your teen not work on Sunday, not just because of the biblical admonition (Exod. 20:8–11), but because the Lord created us with a greater need for rest than for income. If the employer pressures your teenager to work more, work late, or work on Sundays, pursue other options.

- Teach your teen to give a tenth of whatever income he earns to God's work, according to Malachi 3:10: "'Bring the whole tithe into the storehouse . . . and test Me now in this,' says the LORD of hosts, 'if I will not open for you the windows of heaven, and pour out for you a blessing until it overflows'" (NASB). Faithfulness in tithing will provide unforgettable lessons in faith—supernatural lessons that your teen needs to experience firsthand.

- Most parents give their teens some allowance to give them experience in handling money before they are totally on their own. Some parents agree to pay certain expenses, such as clothes. Before the school year starts, you both should sit down and agree on each. Teenagers typically take advantage of the summer months to work full-time, if possible, and save part of that income for spending money during the year. However, paying a teenager to do chores he should be doing anyway (making the bed or paying him for good grades) is probably not a good idea. He should know that there are certain things he's expected to do without remuneration.

- Finally, your teenager needs to learn to prioritize and economize like everyone else who has to work for a living. It is not the end of the world if he can't have everything he wants. In fact, it will benefit him. A little humbling never hurt anyone. Children who never learn to appreciate the value of *other people's* time and money never really mature. They also never know the apostle Paul's secret of contentment or the joy of seeing God provide: "For I have learned, in whatever state I am, to be content. I know how to be abased, and I know how to abound; in any and all circumstances I have learned the secret of facing plenty and hunger, abundance and want. I can do all things in him who strengthens me" (Phil. 4:11–13 RSV).

In the area of expenses, a word about youth mission trips: church youth directors need to be prayerful and intelligent in their planning. Some parents have a hard time understanding why they should spend hundreds of dollars to send their teen cross-country on a mission trip when opportunities to serve abound in their own backyards. Youth directors often protest, "The kids expect to get away." But is this a vacation, or is it to learn service? Parents who are already uneasy about the safety or supervision of their fifteen-year-old on short trips may simply refuse to underwrite his participation on a mission trip. And the popular practice of writing letters to friends and relatives requesting "sponsorship"—asking them for money— has disgusted some families enough to leave a church that endorses this practice. Study the lives of saintly missionaries such as George Müller or Mother Teresa and see how God provided the financial backing for them to do His work. If your teen's activities are truly serving Him, He'll provide the means.

What Could You Say?

To help your teen learn the value of contentment with what he has and how to "stretch a buck," you might say, "Son, a very good way to discern what God has for you is through His financial provision. When God wants you to do or have something, He will provide the means. Let's pray that God will reveal His will for you in this way, and that you will trust Him to provide. Let's also set up a weekly budget to help you manage the money He provides so it will go as far as possible. List every expense for each month, when it occurs and the amount it involves. Then total your expenses and prioritize them. Since your expenses might exceed your allowance, make a list of possible ways to earn additional income. Be willing to work. And you might need to figure out which expenditures to drop. Ask God to provide extra means if He chooses, but thank Him for what He does and does not provide. Once you have your budget and your plan, pass it by me and we'll talk about it. If you fail to curtail your spending to match your income, I'll have to step in and do it for you. Realize, God both gives and withholds things for our good."

Wisdom from God's Word

One of the most valuable gifts you can give teenagers is to teach them to be content with what they have and to trust the Lord to provide for their needs.

My God will supply every need of yours
according to his riches in glory in Christ Jesus.
PHILIPPIANS 4:19 (RSV)

CHAPTER 13
BORROWING

Clothes vanish from closets. Robes disappear from racks. Makeup migrates from bathroom drawers. Jewelry jumps from one bedroom to another, and books walk away by themselves. You wonder if your household has been the target of a thief? Is there a ghost on the loose? No—your daughter Bonnie has become a "borrower." While she freely and without any pang of conscience helps herself to any item she chooses, the rest of the family is reduced to threatening her or pleading with her to return their property. They lock away whatever they don't want to lose. Meanwhile, you are ransacking Bonnie's room for your red scarf in the morning and swallowing antacid when she gets home in the afternoon.

Sometimes this kind of borrowing takes place when teens feel deprived. They borrow something belonging to someone else without permission, but with every intention of returning it after having used it. At other times, borrowing is a result of laziness or thoughtlessness. Regardless, it is a great irritant to the other members of a household (who are the primary targets), especially when items are not returned promptly or in good condition.

What Can You Do?

- Some parents feel that siblings should be encouraged to share with each other since they are members of the same family and thus dependent on each other. This arrangement is good if it is truly voluntary, but all too often one sibling takes advantage of the other's desire to be generous. Thus, you could wind up with one being a disgruntled doormat and the other a frisky freeloader. Establish early on that other people's property is off-limits. If your teenagers have separate bedrooms, they should be taught not to even enter a sibling's room without permission or when that person is absent.

- When siblings share a bedroom, or one is significantly younger than the other, territorial lines tend to blur. Sarah, a sixteen-year-old who shared a bedroom with her younger sister Susie, frequently came home to find her cosmetics or jewelry used or missing. The mother's admonitions to Susie were ineffective in counteracting the lure of the older teenager's possessions. Sarah grew increasingly frustrated and angry about having to replace items Susie had ruined. Finally, the parents bought Sarah a large footlocker for her room in which she stored everything that seemed to interest Susie. Then Sarah padlocked it and kept the key on her key ring.

- As teenagers mature, they need to learn respect for the possessions of others by honoring boundaries. A possession was either handmade and cost someone time, or it was purchased and cost money. Respect for property implies an appreciation for the value of time and money. Therefore, a natural consequence and an effective deterrent to destructive borrowing for teenagers who have any money at all, even if it's just an allowance, is to levy fines. For instance, your ground rules on borrowing might include the following:
    — No borrowing without prior permission.
    — Anything borrowed with permission is to be returned to the owner in pristine condition by the agreed-on time.

— Anything returned late incurs a monetary fine (like five-dollars), payable to the owner.

— Anything returned damaged is to be replaced by the borrower.

— Anything lost, stolen, or destroyed is to be promptly replaced at the borrower's expense.

— Anything borrowed without permission is considered stolen and subject to the above, with an additional, pre-determined penalty (like ten dollars) payable to the owner.

Rules like these are a beginning point, nothing more. Your teenagers need to internalize them so that they become second nature and the problem disappears. If you have to invoke the rules over and over again, then the rules are evidently not working. They may require tweaking to be practical for your household. Before you scrap them altogether, however, consider whether they are being enforced consistently and uniformly. Erratic application is usually the reason for a breakdown in the rules.

- If your teenager is borrowing from family members at will, she's probably borrowing from friends too. Pay attention: Is your daughter eating out frequently when you know she doesn't have the money? She may be mooching off friends. Is her bedroom floor cluttered with unfamiliar clothes? They belong to somebody else. Investigate by asking questions. Your daughter probably will admit that the clothes are Jill's but insist that Jill doesn't mind because "she's got a ton of stuff." In fact, Jill herself may not notice or mind, but the parent paying her clothes bill will be asking, "Where is that outfit I bought you last week?" When Jill replies that your daughter Bonnie has it, her mother fumes, "How many times have I told you not to lend your things to that girl? You never get them back." She insists that Jill ask for them back, and some time later receives a wadded-up bundle to wash and iron. She may even be put in the awkward position of contacting you to explain the matter and ask for replacement or reimbursement. When it gets to this point, it has gone too far.

In a situation such as this, see to it that the borrowed items are promptly returned in excellent condition—by you, if necessary—and borrowed money paid back in full. Then work it out with your daughter to reimburse you.

What Could You Say?

"Bonnie, as you probably know, there's a big difference between *wants* and *needs*. We're committed to providing what you truly need, and it's our joy to provide occasional things that you want. But your habit of borrowing things from others really concerns me. If we aren't providing what you need, then talk to us.

"I don't want you to be seen by your friends as a moocher or freeloader but as a person who respects the property of others and who is responsible enough to carry your own load and pay your own way. Right now you've developed a reputation of not respecting others or their possessions. When you fail to return borrowed items, you are resented by your friends and even your family. From now on, no borrowing unless you talk to me about it first. You will wear clothes from your own closet. And when you are with friends, order only what you have the cash to pay for. If you choose to borrow anyway, your allowance will be suspended. I know you can change, and I want to do whatever I need to do to help you. You have too much to offer others to let this habit come between you and your friends."

Wisdom from God's Word

While Scripture encourages giving, borrowing can quickly become a snare and can tie your teenager to others in a way that damages friendships as well as other relationships. Explain this passage to your teenager:

The borrower is servant to the lender.
PROVERBS 22:7

CHAPTER 14

BACKTALK

You've just walked out of the guest room and hear Lee open the front door.

"Whoa—hold up! Where are you going?"

"I'm going over to Jessica's."

"No, honey, your grandparents should be arriving any time now."

"Why do you always have to tell me what to do?"

(You're stunned. You'd never expected such a response. It's not in your heart to be a dictator!) You remind Lee that this dinner has been set up for months.

"This isn't a home—it's a concentration camp!"

"Lee, your words are inappropriate!" Then with raised right arm in mock salute and a "Heil Hitler," your testy teen abruptly turns and stomps back upstairs.

You thought the war ended years ago, but the verbal bullets continue to come at you. Why is your teenager talking like this?

Talking back is an equal-opportunity enlister among the sexes, but the reasons differ greatly. Boys and girls usually express themselves in predictable ways along gender lines.

Girls tend to cry, whine, throw temper tantrums or use sarcasm. While boys do all this as well (except maybe cry), there is often a confrontational, personally aggressive edge that may be missing in a girl's delivery. This aggression calls for different handling. First, let's talk about girls.

What Can You Do?

- A mother of two teens, ages fifteen and thirteen, relates this experience, "The girls had been sniping at each other. No matter what I said, they were rude to me and each other. So I bought two tubes of travel-sized toothpaste and left them in the dining room. One of the girls asked what they were for. I replied nonchalantly that they were for an experiment we would get to later.

  "Finally, for the fourth day in a row, when one daughter asked about the experiment, I gave both girls a saucer and tube of toothpaste and told them to squeeze out as much toothpaste as they possibly could. Both got right to work, looking at each other's saucer to see who was getting more out or who would finish first.

  "When they finished and looked at me expectantly, I said, 'OK, the *real* contest is to see who can get the most toothpaste *back* in the tube.' The older one began to try desperately, but the younger just pushed the saucer away saying, 'That's impossible.'

  "After a moment, I replied, 'You're right. Words are like toothpaste. Once they come out, you can't get them back in.' I opened my Bible to James 3:10 and read: 'From the same mouth come blessing and cursing . . . this ought not to be so' [RSV]. Then I got up and went back to cooking dinner. No lectures, no pounding.

  "The next day when they began insulting each other, I started making distasteful faces. When they noticed my expression, I said, 'That toothpaste tastes bad.' They got quiet. They got the point!" What a memorable way of breaking a bad habit.
- Many times backtalk is not habitual, but situational, meaning that talking back stems from a distressing situa-

tion—such as a deep disappointment or a painful rejection. Sometimes when an emotional situation erupts into tears or haranguing, the best course is to hold your peace and listen. Be willing to overlook emotional accusations or wild threats—they are probably intended to get your attention. Make certain you hear your teenager's distress call. Let your teenager talk. Don't try to solve anything or answer questions unless specifically asked. Just listen for what is behind the reaction and for what is needed from you. Many times an attentive ear, an embrace, and an assurance of your love are all that are needed to arrive at a better frame of mind.

- If the defiance is more long-term or hostile, your teenager could be developing a real "smart mouth"—talking back to you using sarcasm or even profanity on a regular basis. And although your teen eventually complies with your instructions, it seems that almost every request you make is met with questioning or a hostile verbal response.

  Since undesirable behavior is sometimes extinguished by simply ignoring it, you might first try that approach. As long as your teen ultimately does what you have requested and is not making obscene or vile comments to you, you are being obeyed in the strictest sense of the word.

- Remember to pick your battles, and don't mistake blanks for bullets. That is, teenagers frequently say things they don't mean, either to dramatize their point or just to see how you will respond. Don't take everything they say to heart. And whatever you do, *don't shoot back*. That's the equivalent to fighting fire with gasoline. If you stoop to that level, they will throw it back in your face. If your teenagers do say something hurtful, you could take a long breath and ask, with a grieved spirit, "Son, do you really mean that?" For him to see that you are hurt by his words could appeal to his conscience. Seeing your pain might give him a moment to reflect on what he really wants to say. Keep in mind that he is not your enemy, and you do not want him to see you as his enemy. You are meant to be allies.

- If ignoring the disagreeable talk is not effective, then set the simple but firm rule that when you say "end of discussion," it means there will be no further comments without the repercussion of withdrawn privileges or assigning additional work around the house. Then you walk away.

Language that was utterly taboo a few years ago is now widely heard, especially in the media. Profanity has become such an accepted form of expression in our culture that you should not be overwhelmed if your teen tries it with you. It doesn't mean that he's a hopeless degenerate. Teenagers frequently use expressions whose original meanings are completely unknown to them. One mother who found a note written to her fourteen-year-old son explained, "I was shocked at the extremely coarse language, especially coming from a girl! But it was also sadly amusing. She had misspelled a number of the compound words."

Coarse language should not be tolerated from your teen. Should any profanity be uttered in your presence, make it clear that such language could mean the end of his social contacts for awhile. "I can't have you talk that way. You know that profanity is unacceptable in our home. So tonight, you won't be talking to anyone other than yourself and God." Then immediately remove yourself, depriving him of an audience.

- Sarcasm is such a cutting verbal attack that Oswald Chambers said, "Sarcasm is the weapon of the weak man." It is so humiliating that you must be very careful not to use it with your teenagers. In fact, it's best to eliminate it from your home entirely.

  When you do hear sarcasm, you need to confront it because there may be something else going on in your teen's mind that is being conveyed to you in this veiled way. You need to ask, "What is so wrong that you feel like you have to be sarcastic with me?" Your goal is to redirect the conversation toward a positive end. We all have a deep desire to be understood, even if there is not agreement. For your teen, just to know that you care enough to try to see his point of view can enable him to let go of enough of his anger to meet you halfway. This is what it will take to give your relationship depth. Otherwise, all you have is a shallow existence with your kids, without any effective teaching or learning going on.

What Could You Say?

During a confrontation with your teen about his language, you may want to say something like: "I realize you have opinions about me, and I respect your right to those opinions. I want you to be able to share them with me. But in order for me to hear you, I need for you to express yourself in such a way that I *can* hear you. I have a hard time filtering out a hostile, sarcastic tone of voice in order to get what's really on your heart. Why don't you take a couple of deep breaths and let your anger dissipate a little bit, then we'll see if we can't talk this through. I need you to know that I'm serious enough about this issue to ground you from all activities and privileges until we can work it out. I respect both of us too much to allow disrespectful, angry words to pass between us."

Wisdom from God's Word

Anger begets anger. That's why this is your challenge: not letting your angry teenager spur you to respond in anger. Instead, live out this practical truth that your teen needs to learn to live.

A gentle answer turns away wrath,
but a harsh word stirs up anger.
PROVERBS 15:1

CHAPTER 15
LYING

One Saturday you answer the phone and hear, "Hello, this is Laura's mother. Am I speaking with Claire's mom? I've been talking with my daughter, and I'm afraid I have to let you know that when your daughter told you she spent the night here with Laura, that wasn't true. Laura had told me she was spending the night at *your* house! Actually, what I found out was . . . they both went to a keg party at Chad's house when his parents were out of town."

After thanking her for calling, you hang up in shock, but deep down you're not really surprised. You have come to realize that your daughter has been untruthful on numerous occasions regarding her whereabouts or actions, and your trust level is already quite low. By this time, you feel you cannot believe anything your daughter tells you. You find yourself depressed, angry, and deeply worried.

Lying is the most fundamental of wrongs in that it strikes at the heart of any relationship. No other disobedience can be carried out without a covering lie. No teen is going to say, "Hey, Mom, I'm going to a keg party at Chad's while his parents are gone. I don't know when I'll be home." Parents dread the discovery of lying (usually there is a pattern, as lies rarely come singly) because they want to believe their teenagers simply would not lie to them. In fact, you should give your teen the benefit of the doubt . . . until the evidence says otherwise. If you start seeing inconsistencies, you must not look away. Start digging, painful as it may be, to discover the dishonesty.

What Can You Do?

- First, be glad you found out. Some parents are so clueless that they never figure out what is going on under their noses, rendering themselves useless to guide or protect. The mother of one eighteen-year-old commented, "I am grateful to have such a good relationship with my daughter that she talks to me. However, she also talks to me about what some of her friends are doing behind their parents' backs. These kids get away with everything because their parents never question them or check up on them. It's hard to know what to say when I see the parents." In this case, there's little you can say without betraying your teen's confidences. If those parents overlook the evidence right in front of their faces, they're not going to listen to you anyway.

- I know other parents who pray that whenever their teens lie to them or do anything they should not do, they *will* get caught. The point is not to be hard on them, but to protect them from the delusion that they can get away with something and suffer no consequences. An old adage is true: "Plant a thought, harvest an action; plant an action, harvest a habit; plant a habit, harvest a character; plant a character, harvest your destiny."

There are patterns of lying that are difficult to figure out, such as lying about little, inconsequential things. If this is happening, find out what purpose is being served by lying. When I was a teenager, I lied a great deal. I'm not proud of that, but it helps me understand how someone can get caught in that trap. For a while, I did not feel guilty about it. It was a part of my lifestyle well into my twenties, until I finally got to the root of my compulsion to lie.

I remember sitting in my car one night thinking about this. I really wanted to change, but I had no concept of why I was being untruthful. As I thought about my earliest recollection of lying, I saw that it always involved protecting my mother. I lied to procure peace in our home. Out of loyalty to loved ones, I lied and did not have a guilty conscience about it for years.

Only after becoming a Christian did I see that one characteristic of Christ is truth. Jesus not only told the truth; He was truth incarnate. Therefore, I needed to honor the truth and accept the consequences that might come with speaking the truth. Perhaps most helpful to me was repeatedly praying this prayer: "Lord, may I see sin as You see it. May I hate sin as You hate it."

- In most homes there is an authority figure, someone with the right to set the rules. Unfortunately, the authority may turn into a kind of dictator. But even in a benevolent dictatorship, teens can feel a sense of powerlessness. That's where manipulation comes in. Manipulation is a tool used by a weaker person seeking to control a stronger person by deception. An integral part of manipulation is lying. When parents encounter evidence of pervasive lying, they need to examine whether their system of rules makes the teenager feel so powerless that lying is an attempt to exert some measure of control over her circumstances. If this is the case, parents might consider empowering their daughter with more choices—only after the necessary repercussions have convinced her that lying is not the best way to get what she wants.

Some teens lie to protect themselves from suffering undesirable consequences for unapproved or questionable activities, as in the keg party caper. Other teens try to do things without the knowledge of their parents in an attempt to become separate individuals. Still another reason people lie is deeply rooted in their need for significance. In this case, a student would claim to have made better grades than he actually did, or boast of certain athletic or macho feats that he didn't do.

When you have ascertained what you believe is the real reason for your teen's pattern of lying, do some self-evaluation. Is your teenager fearful of you? Are you being too strict, overly rigid, uncompromising, unreasonable, or unapproachable? Consult an objective observer who knows both you and your teenager to get an unbiased opinion.

When you are prepared to talk to your teen about the situation, start with an appeal to her conscience. Express your deep disappointment in being deceived by someone you love so much—someone in whom you had placed your trust. Explain that seeds of distrust have been sown in all of her relationships. You cannot help but distrust her friends because they supported her dishonesty. The repercussion is that your teen will not enjoy the freedom or the privacy she had previously enjoyed. All activities will be monitored by you or someone you trust until trustworthiness is reestablished. Understand that it's your teen's responsibility to make a plan to regain your trust. She is to present a plan that is acceptable to you, and then carry it out faithfully.

What Could You Say?

You might say: "I know that lying sometimes seems a viable way out of a difficult situation, but it ends up destroying relationships. If you keep doing it, it will cost you the relationships you value most. When no one can trust you, and you can't even trust yourself, your self-respect goes out the window. Deceit also torpedoes your enjoyment of your relationship with God. And above all, I don't want that to happen to you.

"Our being able to trust you is the basis of your freedoms within our family. It's up to you to figure out how you are going to become trustworthy and regain those freedoms. Until then, you are grounded from all parties. I am here to help you in any way I can, but I can't make you be truthful. You have to do that on your own. When you're ready to discuss a plan that you think will help, let me know, and we'll talk about it."

Wisdom from God's Word

What teenager doesn't want to be free! Tell your teen: lying will keep you in bondage, but it's truth that sets you free.

The LORD detests lying lips,
but he delights in men who are truthful.
PROVERBS 12:22

CHAPTER 16
OBJECTIONABLE MUSIC

You walk into the house, nudging the door open with your foot because your arms are loaded with four full grocery sacks. Immediately upon entering, you are blasted backward by the volume of heavy-metal guitar riffs. The walls are shaking, and dishes on the countertop are vibrating. "Matt!" you shout, trying to be heard. "MATTHEW!" It's hopeless. Matt doesn't even realize your presence until—hands flat over your ears—you make your way to the CD player and turn off the blaring sound. Matt looks up in surprise from the couch as you close your eyes in relief. Then, straining to maintain your composure, you pick up the empty CD case and calmly ask, "What are you listening to?"

Questionable music has become a conflict in almost every household where teenagers reside. Generational differences are never more apparent than in the music each prefers and the volume at which it is played. I was amused at one mother who shared, "I recently looked through the journal I keep about Clint and came across the following prayer he prayed a couple of years ago. . . . 'Lord, help me even when I get to be a teenager and I'm a juvenile delinquent to still have a good relationship with my parents, so I won't turn into one of those people who listen to really loud music and ruin their hearing.' So far, the Lord has answered this prayer. His tastes lean toward country music, and he doesn't like it loud. It seems his hearing is safe for the time being."

This boy is not typical. Today's teenagers seem to like screeching guitars and grating vocals, and they like it LOUD. It's one thing to ask them to turn it down, which they will, if they want the privilege of listening to it at all. But what if the lyrics themselves are downright objectionable?

What Can You Do?

- Don't react out of ignorance. Listen closely to the words on the CDs. If the words are not discernible, read the inserts. Since CDs with explicit lyrics or profanities are required to carry a parental advisory sticker, look at every CD your teen buys. You can also check out the lyrics of almost any CD by looking up that artist's web site on the Internet.

  If you discover CDs containing lyrics you find offensive, sit down with your teenager . . . with lyrics in hand. That way, should he protest that "there's nothing wrong with the music I listen to," you will have something specific to talk about.

- Offer your teen some alternatives. There has been an explosion in the variety of Christian music available, which attracts teens by the thousands—contemporary music styles with lyrics that could be straight from the Psalms. Help your teen explore these options to find a sound he likes with a message you like. If he goes to the music store to sell back the objectionable CDs, you might offer to pay for one or two Christian CDs to start his new collection. (One warning: should the objectionable CDs be spiritually oppressive, you should considering destroying them.)

- Be aware that even after you have put all these safeguards into place, your teen will still be able to access or download for free almost any music he wants through computer programs. While the wrangling goes on over the legality of this music-sharing software, these popular, easily accessible programs are not going away. You need to handle this as you would any other computer-related problem.

What Could You Say?

As in any conflict in which you are trying to find common ground, lead in love: "Although we won't always like the same things, I will always love you. But I can't find anything to like in this music. What do you think they mean by this?" Show him specifically what you object to and wait for a response (which will probably be noncommittal).

"I am sincerely concerned about your listening to messages like this and filling your mind with these kinds of thoughts. Your mind is like any other container . . . what goes in is what comes out. That is, if you fill your mind with garbage, then garbage is going to start controlling your thoughts and coming out your mouth. God designed you for just the opposite. He wants you to fill your mind with pure and righteous thoughts so your words and actions honor Him. I mean, put yourself in my shoes for a minute. Would you want your son going around singing words like this?

"Ultimately, it's your decision what you fill your mind with. Because I love you, I want to encourage you to keep your mind pure, regardless of what everybody else is doing. It's inevitable that what you listen to will shape your attitude, and your attitude will shape your actions. I want you to stay clear of the traps of a bad attitude because that's only going to hurt you in the long run. I also do not want to subject anyone else in this house to words like this. Therefore, this music is not to be played in our house. If it is, your CDs will be confiscated. I have confidence you will respect this decision because we both know it's right in God's sight.

"Since we are discussing objectionable music, this might be a good time to say a word about offensive posters." I guarantee, he will initially protest after you ask him to remove his favorite hard rock ensemble commanding center stage over his bed. Explain, "The same principles that applied to what you listen to apply to what you take in visually . . . garbage in, garbage out! Even if you do not agree with me on this matter, when you have your own home, you will have full authority over what hangs on the walls. I want you to be able to express your individuality in your own bedroom, but I believe you are mature enough to understand it's a matter of principle. And I am confident you will honor what I believe is right in God's sight."

Wisdom from God's Word

The apostle Paul's counsel is practical and pertinent for today's teenage culture. He helps us know what to let into our minds, which then ultimately guards our hearts.

Whatever is true, whatever is noble, whatever is right,
whatever is pure, whatever is lovely, whatever is admirable—
if anything is excellent or praiseworthy—
think about such things.
PHILIPPIANS 4:8

CHAPTER 17

MISUSE OF MEDIA

You walk into the family room while Trevor, your teenager, is watching a popular, prime-time comedy show. You're not really paying attention until a person on the show utters one of the most obscene remarks you've ever heard, and the room fills with canned laughter.

You've reached your limit. You're sick of the sexual sewage spewing out over the airwaves through TV and CDs, in magazines and movies, pop concerts and posters, all directly into Trevor's brain. Obscenity, disrespect, and irreverence have become so pervasive in today's entertainment that it sometimes seems the only way to get away from it all is to find an uninhabited island on which to raise your teens. But what if you can't find your own island retreat?

What Can You Do?

- As we lump together the use of television, radio, VCR, DVD, and computer, the same principle applies: your teen must respect the rights of the others who live in your house. Certain radio stations need to be off-limits—not necessarily because of the music, but because of the talk.

Many DJs take delight in offending on the air, but don't let them form a fan club in your home!

- Offensive television shows or movies should not be viewed—period. One family I know simply prohibits the playing of any R-rated movies in the house. "We might miss some good movies, but we'll survive. What I won't survive is wading through all the trashy movies and fighting about which ones are acceptable," the mom explained.

- The computer has spawned a revolution of its own in our culture. For education, research, entertainment, and business potential, no other medium approaches it. No other medium carries the potential dangers either. First, many computer games feature not only graphic violence and bloodshed but also overtly satanic and sadomasochistic imagery. Pick up any *PC Gamer* magazine and look at the ads. Watch the demos of the games your son wishes to buy or rent. Check the game's package description, including its rating, which is supplied by the Entertainment Software Rating Board and is displayed on the front of each game. The ratings are:

  — Early Childhood (EC)—suitable for children age 3 and up.

  — Everyone (E)—suitable for persons age 6 and up. May contain some crude language and minimal violence.

  — Teen (T)—suitable for persons age 13 and up. May contain strong language, suggestive themes, and some violence.

  — Mature (M)—suitable for persons age 17 and up. May include violence, adult language, and mature sexual themes.

  — Adults Only (AO)—suitable for adults only. May include graphic sex, extreme violence, and strong language. Should not be sold or rented to persons under 18.

  — Rating Pending (RP)—the game has been submitted to the ESRB for rating.

For any game you have qualms about, explain your objections once and then exert your parental authority. Say no.

- Internet chat rooms pose another problem. Anyone can get online and have real-time, instant, anonymous conversations with a bunch of total strangers. It's like opening your telephone line to anyone in the world who happens to want to talk at the moment. The anonymity and impersonal nature of words on a screen breed unrestrained language. Even when those conversing know each other, it can get out of hand. As an example, below is an excerpt from an actual online conversation between a fifteen-year-old boy ("Viper") and a classmate ("Random"), given to me by "Viper's" mother:

  Viper: u must have threatened to kill me 50 times

  Random: yea . . . but that isn't half as many as i've threatened to kill everyone

  Viper: lol [laughing out loud] so does that actually mean anything or r u actually going to kill me?

  Random: i'm actually gonna kill u

  Viper: oh, ok

  Random: no . . . no . . . i'm serious

  Viper: i know u r

  Random: once i become a terrorist. i'm dead serious about becoming one

  Viper: i know

  Random: good

  Viper: so how do u plan to kill me?

  Random: hmmm . . . u'll find out . . . but i swear on gauna that u can count on it

  "Viper" has been banned from further online conversations, by the way.

The more prevalent problem of chat rooms is "virtual sex," or graphic descriptions of sex play, which can lead to further complications. One set of parents became suspicious when their son began buying calling cards to talk long distance with a girl he met in a teen chat room, which was supposedly monitored to keep out explicit talk. The son had obtained the girl's telephone number online and began spending long periods of time on the phone with her. By accidentally picking up an extension during one of these conversations, the father overheard graphic sex talk. The son was immediately grounded from both the telephone and the computer. In time, he regained his computer privileges, but only under supervision. The parents retain the right to read any of his messages or view his E-mail.

Besides the lure of virtual sex, the other dangerous aspect of chat rooms is the highly publicized use pedophiles or sexual predators make of them to lure teens to meeting them, usually at a motel. Molestation or rape is not the worst that can happen here. Newspapers have carried graphic accounts of murders stemming from online meetings.

Probably the number one threat of the Internet, however, is the proliferation of easily accessible, hard-core pornography. One counselor noted that the demand for counseling teens addicted to Internet pornography has exploded in recent years. Software programs that supposedly block dangerous sites can be continually circumvented by ingenious pornographers. One student doing a report typed *gecko* in the search engine. The brightly colored screen on the first site it displayed read, "The following HOT HOT HOT pix are for ADULTS ONLY. So don't click 'continue' unless you're over 18!" Be aware of the bait for sexually curious teens . . . be aware, be alert, be alarmed.

- For any danger with the computer, the only adequate precaution is parental supervision. Counselors strongly recommend against children having computers with modems in their bedrooms. Teens should not have unrestricted, private access to the Internet any more than they should to movie theaters. Parents should insist on the right to monitor their children's E-mail inboxes for unsolicited porn advertisements. If you have any doubts about where your child has been on the Web, check your Internet history of site visits. You can't stop your teen from knowing more about the Internet than you, but if you're at his elbow the whole time he's on, you're bound to learn something!

- For all these media, the problem may be not that your teen is abusing them, but that he spends every waking moment either on the computer, in front of the TV, or with headphones attached to his head. One mother who became concerned about her son's electronic IVs finally declared two hours every school night to be under an "electronic blackout." Anything that required electricity or batteries (lights excluded) was turned off during those two hours. Her son fought this restriction energetically for a while, but his grades in English improved noticeably.

What Could You Say?

"Son, I want the very best for you and am grateful for all you've learned through the computer. I'm not trying to restrict your activities just to be hard on you or to be a dictator. I know we both realize how impressionable the mind can be . . . it absorbs and stores everything it sees and hears. This is why God tells us in the Bible, we are 'transformed by the renewing of our minds.' This is why we need to closely guard and protect our minds from anything ungodly. I want you to use and enjoy the computer, as well as other means of entertainment, but we need to establish accountability. Let's both give it some thought and see what we can come up with." (Be sure to follow through by talking about the issue before a week has passed.)

Wisdom from God's Word

The mind of your teenager needs to be challenged to move away from worldly thoughts and worldly things. Teens need to know that God can free anyone trapped in this web—the Worldwide Web—by totally transforming their minds.

Do not conform any longer to the pattern of this world,
but be transformed by the renewing of your mind.
Then you will be able to test and approve what God's will is—
his good, pleasing and perfect will.
ROMANS 12:2

CHAPTER 18

TELEPHONE ABUSE

You're at home, expecting an important business call that should have come twenty minutes earlier. Out of concern, you pick up the receiver—and hear your daughter's voice. You interrupt the conversation saying, "Holly, I'm so sorry, but I'm expecting a call. Will you please hang up the phone?"

"Sure, Mom," she chirps. So, you hang up, but five minutes pass and the phone still does not ring. Tentatively, you pick up the receiver and hear Holly's voice again.

"Holly! You said you were getting off the line!" you say.

"Gee, Mom, keep your shirt on. I'm hanging up," she says. Once more you take her at her word, but five minutes later, with mounting suspicion, you check the line again—only to hear Holly's mellifluous voice going strong. It's time for a new tactic.

What Can You Do?

- What if your home telephone is being monopolized by your teenager? Many families resolve the problem by buying a separate telephone line for their teen. But as often happens, if your teen's friends call on her line and can't reach her, they will call her on your line. Do you play secretary for your teen or do you invest in yet more technology (such as call waiting) to achieve some peace?

- Some parents have determined to do neither. Rather than be controlled by the demands of technology or of their teen, they feel it will serve her best if she learns courtesy and time management. They restrict her use of the phone by insisting on:
    - — no calls during dinner
    - — no calls during study time
    - — no calls after 10:00 P.M.
    - — no interruptive operator assisted emergency calls from her friends (unless it is a true emergency).

  Failure to follow these guidelines results in losing telephone privileges for a certain amount of time.

- If your teen shares a phone line with anyone else, there should be an automatic time limit—say, twenty minutes—on all calls. If this is an ongoing rule, it can help preclude fights over having the phone tied up when someone else is expecting a call. But you should also make it clear that she is expected to surrender the phone immediately for someone else's emergency (even if she does not consider the need urgent) because she will have emergencies for which she will expect immediate use of the phone. This is a great opportunity for learning the practicality of the Golden Rule. Any unauthorized long-distance calls that she makes or any charges she incurs for frills (such as three-way calling) she will have to pay for herself.

- Caller ID is another technology that has greatly cut down on the number of harassing and obscene phone calls. But again, not everyone wishes to spend money for it when good manners should suffice. You can teach your teen early on to identify herself when placing calls.

- The issue of cell phones can get even stickier since the cell phone user is charged for calls she receives as well as calls she places. Partial minutes are rounded up, and exceeding the minutes on one's plan can run up substantial charges. Still, you may want your teen to carry the phone for safety reasons. One solution is to keep the cell phone number a closely guarded secret. Only you and essential others, such as siblings, should have it. When giving her the phone, you need to cover the ground rules for its use: check-in calls to you and emergency calls only. When she "forgets" this rule (as she probably will, at first) she will have to pay the penalties herself for exceeding the minutes. Your ground rules should also cover cell phone etiquette.

What Could You Say?

To keep your teenager from monopolizing the telephone, explain, "Gina, I know you enjoy talking with your friends. I want you to be able to talk with them. I also know you need to demonstrate respect for the rest of the family by keeping some rules for phone usage. If you break the rules, your phone privileges will be totally revoked for the next two days. That's not what I want for you, but it's your choice whether they are revoked or not. I want you to be courteous and not continue a phone conversation when someone else in the family needs to make a phone call. Of course, the number one rule is that you not use the phone during homework time or after bedtime. Your father or I will answer the phone then and take messages for you, but it's best if you tell your friends not to call during homework time or after 10:00 P.M. Also, during school nights you need to limit your phone conversations to 20 minutes. On weekends you can talk longer as long as you release the phone when someone else needs to use it. If someone calls while you are on the telephone, you will need to find out who it is and release the phone if the call is for your father or me. If the call is for your brother or sister, you will need to limit the rest of your call to five minutes. You can just take a message if the person being called is not here.

"Make it clear to your friends that under no circumstances are they to make an emergency phone call through the operator in an attempt to talk with you. There may be times when your father or I will ignore call waiting if we are on an important call and do not want to be interrupted. That is something you, on the other hand, are not allowed to do. There are just some privileges that go with paying the bill. I don't want you talking on the telephone all night and neglecting your father and me. We enjoy your company too much for that."

Wisdom from God's Word

Teaching your teenager to treat others with respect in regard to the telephone is not only helpful, but it also follows the Golden Rule:

Always treat others as you would
like them to treat you.
MATTHEW 7:12 (NEB)

CHAPTER 19

DRIVING DANGEROUSLY

It's Monday, and you're feeling it. So many things have gone wrong today that you can't imagine how it could get worse . . . until you get a phone call. "Uh, Dad? It's Lane. Uh, Dad, I need you to come pick me up at the corner of Mockingbird and Central. I had a little fender-bender. I'm not hurt. It was just a really minor thing. No, I can't drive it, the right front fender's, like, crumpled around the tire. Police? Uh, uh yeah . . . a ticket for speeding, and uh, following too closely. But, don't worry, I'll pay for it. No problem. Uh, Dad, by the way, I'm gonna need your car to pick up Lisa tonight."

There's no more volatile combination than teens and cars, but our largely suburban lifestyle makes mobility for teenagers almost a necessity for busy families. Be prepared when, as inevitably happens, your teen proves himself irresponsible with the family car.

What Can You Do?
- One Chicago family's experience is instructive here. The mother writes: "One day in the mail I discovered a letter from the Secretary of State. It informed us that our teen-

ager had received a speeding ticket and, should he receive just one more, there would be stiff legal penalties. Just a friendly note from the Secretary of State! They must know that teenagers don't divulge that information. Our son certainly did not.

"I showed the letter to my husband and we set our son down at the kitchen table for a lengthy talk. He admitted to getting the ticket five months ago. He had paid the fine secretly, hoping to avoid a parental confrontation. Of course, he did not realize that the fine was only part of the official consequences for his speeding.

"Other consequences came swiftly: we grounded him from using the car for a specified period of time. He also was grounded from certain privileges for an even longer period of time. The biggest consequence, however, was the one he brought on himself by his ignorance of the law. Had he owned up to his mistake, we could have shown him the appropriate means to handle the ticket.

"Notice his way:
1. A $95 fine.
2. The loss of his 'Good Student Driver' discount on our car insurance. He now owes us the difference that we must pay, which is $153.
3. The violation is now on his driving record (hence the discontinuation of the discount on insurance).
4. One more speeding ticket could lead to a two-year suspension of his driver's license.
5. The most drastic possibility is that his license could be revoked.
6. This hangs over his head for two years.

"With our guidance:
1. He would have chosen to go to court, thus paying a lesser fine.
2. The violation would not have gone on his driving record.
3. The 'Good Student Driver' discount would have remained in effect.
4. His license would not be suspended should he get another ticket.

5. The threat of a revoked license would not be quite as likely.

6. The 'reprimand' period would be less than two years. "This lesson cost him over $200!"

- It stands to reason that whatever damage a teen driver causes to a vehicle, he pays out of his own pocket (if he was at fault). The shock of discovering that replacing a bumper costs $800 to $1200—conservatively—will make cautious drivers out of most cash-strapped teens. (Some parents have put a bumper sticker on their teen's vehicle that says, "How's my driving? Call [parent's phone number]." While this is excruciatingly embarrassing to a teen, it can also be a deterrent to dangerous hot-doggers.)

What Could You Say?

"Son, I'm deeply grateful to God for protecting you from injury. It sounds like you or someone else could have been seriously hurt considering the damage done to your car. I'm grateful you will not have to live with the devastating consequences if that had happened. I think God has given us both a wake-up call, and we need to heed His warning. Breaking the law and wrecking your car says to me that you need to take more responsibility for your actions and have more maturity under your belt before you get behind the wheel again. It will be a hardship on your Mom and me to provide all your transportation, but we will manage. The important thing is that you learn from this mistake. We'll talk later about how you're going to pay for your tickets, for repairs on the car, and when you will attend a defensive driving course. I'm confident that you can become more responsible and regain our trust. Devise a plan and bring it to us within three days.

Wisdom from God's Word

Just as God's laws are boundaries to keep believers in line, civil laws are boundaries that keep all of us in line. Teens who cross over the line need to be on a correction course. Ultimately, God's laws are safeguards for our lives.

Submit yourselves to every human institution for the sake of the Lord. . . . For it is the will of God that by your good conduct you should put ignorance and stupidity to silence.
1 PETER 2:13, 15 (NEB)

CHAPTER 20
BREAKING CURFEW

Danny is out on his first solo date. You know the girl and like her; you know where they're going and what they'll be doing. You've covered the ground rules thoroughly. But you're still a little uneasy. You also know Danny's tendency to push against the boundaries. He doesn't think he *breaks* rules, he just *bends* them a little. His curfew tonight is 11:00 P.M., but you're not confident that he'll take the time seriously. Sure enough, he walks in, smiling and relaxed, at 11:10. Your response to this is important.

What Can You Do?

- Curfew can be the number one conflict between parents and teens. The teens want to be out at night, and their parents want them in. In the case of a broken curfew, consequences are called for because if Danny gets away with coming in a little late this time, he'll think nothing of coming in a lot later the next time. Still, you don't want to go ballistic over ten minutes.
- When setting curfews with your son, establish the consequences down to the minute. That way there is no room

for ambiguity or charges of unfairness. For instance, you might agree that for every ten minutes he comes in past curfew, the next curfew will be shortened by thirty minutes. Get his agreement before he leaves, and yes, you may have to synchronize watches!

If he complains about hair-splitting, emphasize that the reason for exactness is to make sure you are fair about it. If he is as much as ten minutes late, he will know without being told that his curfew next time will be 10:30 P.M. If he makes it on time then, you can reestablish his curfew at 11:00 P.M.

- If your son is developing a habit of breaking curfew, you will have to consider stronger measures, such as limiting his activities to only those events to which you or another responsible person can drive him. On the other hand, you could decide to eliminate the activities that give him the most trouble.

In all fairness though, you need to recognize that some activities, such as school athletics, at times run longer than expected. You might have to say something like, "I expect you to come home immediately after the football game." If he fails to do so, then he loses his privilege to go to the next football game.

- Admittedly, there are going to be times when the issue of curfew becomes moot. For instance, theater or band rehearsals are notorious for lasting into the wee hours; and if your teen wishes to participate, he will simply have no control over when he gets home. This is hard on parents who have to get up to go to work in the morning. About the only thing you can do is become involved in the activity's booster club. Not only will you have an opportunity to observe the inner workings of the group, you will have a schedule for projected late nights. Since school districts have rules about how long directors can keep students on school nights, you need to be informed. Then you will know if your son is where he is supposed to be, doing what he is supposed to do.

What Could You Say?

You could say something like, "I know you want to go out with your friends on your own, and I want that for you too. But it is important that both of us know you can be trusted to keep your word. And that means coming home when you say you will. I need to know that I can count on you to do what you say. If you're late, I'll start to worry; and if I'm worried, I'll start calling around to check up on you. I don't think you want me calling other parents at 2:00 in the morning!

"If getting home on time proves to be difficult for you, we'll shorten your curfew by thirty minutes for every ten minutes you are late. Then we'll return to your original curfew after you make the new curfew once. If you continue to come in late, I will have to go back to driving the car for you until you've developed the discipline to keep your curfew. If you can think of a better way to get yourself home on time, let me know, and we'll talk about it."

Wisdom from God's Word

One of the most trying lessons for teenagers has to do with time: how to be conscious of time when you're with friends who have no curfew. While time constraints can feel painful, in the long-run they produce peace.

No discipline seems pleasant at the time, but painful.
Later on, however, it produces a harvest of righteousness
and peace for those who have been trained by it.
HEBREWS 12:11

CHAPTER 21

SNEAKING OUT

Your fifteen-year-old daughter, Amber, has developed a crush on a nineteen-year-old high school dropout. You are adamantly opposed to her seeing him and have told her so. One Saturday she comes to ask permission to go to a party where you know she will see this boy. You refuse, and she runs to her room crying.

Hours later, in the middle of the night, you get up for a drink of water. Vague suspicions have crept into your mind; you go to your daughter's bedroom and quietly open the door. Amber's bed is empty. She is gone.

Some teens seem to have an urgent need to test boundaries, including physical boundaries. There is something almost irresistible and empowering about climbing out a window after-hours. Welcome to the ranks of parents with teenagers who won't stay put for the night!

What Can You Do?

- A forty-year-old woman confided: "When I was seventeen, I often climbed out of my bedroom window at night to meet a married man. When my parents got wind of the fact that I was going out the window, my dad bolted the screen shut. Other than that, they never said a word to me. That didn't stop me, of course. I just started using the back door. But if we'd had a fire that blocked the hallway, I would have fried!"

She reflected, "I know what *would* have stopped me: if they had just confronted me about it. It really would have made a difference for them to say, 'We love you too much to let you destroy your life doing this.' I would have respected that. I knew that what I was doing was wrong, but I didn't have the moral backbone to stop. I needed their help." Bottom line, she wanted limits with love. She got the limits, but not the love . . . but the limits didn't work.

- Prohibition is not the only stance a caring parent can take. The choices are not just two—limits or liberty. You can be creatively proactive . . . especially if you see the signs of "sneakiness" lurking around the corner:
    — Take your teens to the emergency room at the county hospital on a Friday or Saturday night to observe from 11:00 P.M. to 5:00 A.M.
    — Do computer research together on high school dropouts covering employment and criminal statistics.
    — Ride around in a police patrol car during the late night shift on a weekend night.
    — Research the statistics on violent crimes committed between dusk and dawn during weekends.
    — Attend a community service program and neighborhood watch program on violent crime protection.
    — Check newspaper stories for incidents involving crimes committed at night against teens in your city. Consider meeting with one or more victims who will share their story with your teen.
- In contrast, a Denver mom relates this experience: "One evening our fourteen-year-old daughter had two girlfriends staying overnight. At 2:00 in the morning, these girls decided to call a taxi to go over to a boy's house. A neighbor called in a complaint of prowlers to the sheriff.

He came out to investigate while the taxi was still sitting in front of our house. The sheriff asked the taxi driver who he was waiting for, and he gave them our address and phone number. The sheriff called us to ask if we had requested a cab. I said no, but then I got suspicious.

"In between the time the sheriff called and I got downstairs to check on the girls, they had snuck out the back door, got in the taxi, and took off. I called the sheriff's office. When they finally contacted the driver, he had already dropped off his fares at an intersection near downtown. I called both of the other girls' parents, and we all got in our cars to circle the intersection. The police were also out looking for them.

"Around 4 A.M., one mom followed a taxi all the way back to our house, where 'Guess Who' got out. Their parents came for them immediately, and the next morning all the girls and parents met at our house.

"My husband, an administrator of a Christian organization, then proceeded to 'investigate' the incident with clipboard in hand. As it turned out, the girls did go to this boy's house, a fourteen-year-old who had two other boys sleeping over. My husband, taking notes on his clipboard, grilled the girls individually about everything, including who was there, what they had drunk or eaten, and who was wearing what. The girls admitted that they entered the boy's house through his bedroom window, watched a movie, ate snacks, and drank pop, then left again through the bedroom window. My husband then called the three boys to our house and proceeded to 'investigate' the matter with them as well. They were scared spitless! He directed them to confess the incident to their parents and call him confirming that they had done so within twenty-four hours, or he would call the parents himself. All the boys complied."

What Could You Say?

A teen who sneaks out of the house is not a rare exception. But a confrontation with love and limits is. You will be a hero in their hearts as you learn how to enforce limits with love.

You might say, "We know you're growing up and making more and more of your own decisions. One day you will be making all of the decisions that affect your life, but as parents who love you, we still have the responsibility to guide you and discipline you for all inappropriate, dangerous, or harmful behavior.

"Sneaking out of your room at night and going somewhere we don't want you to go with someone we don't want you dating are all totally unacceptable. We are hurt and disappointed that you would blatantly defy us like this. We knew you were upset that we couldn't give you permission to go to the party, but we trusted you to honor our wishes. Until we are convinced that we can trust you in the future, you are grounded. If you continue to defy us, you will remain grounded. Sneak out again, and we will call the police. These are non-negotiables, not because we don't care about you, but because we do care about you."

What happened in the case of the daughter from Denver? Her mother shares the rest of the story.

"As for punishment, our daughter was grounded with no outside activities besides church for two months (as they were gone for two hours), with a mandatory good attitude. After four weeks, we lifted her grounding for good behavior. She indicates now that the worst part of the whole thing was the investigation via clipboard. My husband's handling it in an official manner gave all the kids an appreciation for the seriousness of the matter, not just for their deception, but for putting themselves at risk by being out in a taxi in the middle of the night."

Wisdom from God's Word

One of the things that causes the most concern about teenagers is their abundant lack of common sense when it comes to heading into harm's way. Discipline can be an effective deterrent—a safeguard for every teen.

> *Discipline your son, for in that there is hope;*
> *do not be a willing party to his death.*
> PROVERBS 19:18

PERSONAL
BOUNDARIES

The boundaries regarding your teen's actual body or person can be the most disconcerting of all for parents since it is in this area where the process of independence first asserts itself. You don't want your daughter looking like a streetwalker nor your son a thug, but teens greatly resent suggestions from their parents regarding their physical appearance and personal interests. Negotiating this cold war with your relationship still intact calls for exercising the most diplomacy you can muster. Ask God for discernment and his guidance as you seek to bond with your teen through these personal boundaries.

CHAPTER 22
CONFLICTS OVER CLOTHES

You stand at your sixteen-year-old daughter's bedroom door and knock. "Megan! I'm ready to go. If you're going to the mall with me, you have to come now."

Megan promptly opens the door. "OK. I'm ready."

Your mouth opens, your jaw drops, your eyes widen as you gaze at her in disbelief. Megan is wearing a skimpy halter-top with no bra, very short cut-off jeans, sandals, and toe rings. You can't imagine her wearing such a get-up in the privacy of her own bedroom, much less in public. Megan regards the look on your face and puckers her heavily glossed lips stubbornly, primed for another fight over her use of make-up and choice of clothes. Something must be done and you know it.

Clothes are more an issue with girls than with boys. Boys generally want their clothes to fit in with the group they hang with. The more extreme styles are often regulated by the school. Obscene t-shirts, chains, torn clothing, and sagging pants are generally prohibited. Thus the boys' opportunities to shock with their clothing are limited for the most part.

Girls have another shopping agenda. As they reach adolescence, an important criterion in their selection of clothes is displaying their physical charms. Thus they will test you (and the school guidelines) with short skirts, short shorts, tube tops, spaghetti straps, bare midriffs, and plunging necklines. Back-to-school shopping can degenerate into a tug of war between a mother bent on decency and a daughter bent on popularity.

Cost, too, becomes an important factor. The most popular clothes that the most popular people wear are, of course, the most expensive. Teens can be extremely demeaning about someone else's clothes. Some students feel that not having a closet full of the most desired labels will impair their social status. For this reason, an increasing number of public schools are adopting the private-school practice of requiring uniforms. Many teens hate them, but they are a great leveler—no one can make fun of anyone's clothes when everyone is wearing the same thing. Teachers love them because a whole class in uniforms makes for a neat, scholarly appearance, contributing to a sense of order. Principals love them because there is no time wasted on dealing with inappropriately dressed students. And parents love them for the hassle-free shopping and dressing each morning. Although there may be a significant cash outlay at the beginning of the year, uniforms consistently prove to be a better value than mall clothes. Many schools even have hand-me-down programs from graduating students to incoming students.

What Can You Do?

- If your daughter attends a school where freedom of dress is sacred, and your expectations on what she will wear differ widely from hers, study the school's dress code before you ever set foot in a store. It is probably very specific about what is allowed, and administrators are far more strict about the students' adherence to it in September than in May.
- Armed with the dress code, go through your daughter's closet with her to see what she has to start the year and

what she needs. Make a shopping list as to specific items needed for non-school activities as well. Set a budget. Check the newspaper for sales; brace yourself; take your daughter; and go.

- If you and your daughter are adventurous, it could be really fun to give her some cash and turn her loose in a secondhand store. Certain types of vintage clothing are always in vogue, and present a wealth of opportunities to be creative and original, not to mention thrifty. It is also a wonderful experience for your daughter to discover that bargain hunting is fun, and treasures hide in the most unlikely surroundings.

What Could You Say?

If Megan presents herself in skimpy, inappropriate attire, you say, "Megan, many times I've seen you exercise sound judgment and I could respect your decisions, but I can't bear seeing you have so little respect for yourself by dressing like this. Sweetheart, you have no idea how it makes you look. It isn't flattering to you. One of my major concerns is that the way you are dressing right now demonstrates a blatant disregard for the moral character of your male friends. I will assume you don't understand what a moral snare it is to guys who struggle to remain sexually pure in their minds. It's important to both of us that you be respected. Honey, you have ten minutes to change. Hurry, so we can get on the road." (If she balks, say, "Megan, maybe this isn't the best day. Perhaps we can try again next week. I think we'll have a great day together. I look forward to spending time with you shopping for school clothes.")

In the car on the way, you might pleasantly lay out some ground rules: "OK, honey, you know what we need and how much we have to spend. I'm going to let you pick out the clothes. Whatever you find that is on our list and that you can wear to school I'll put in the cart until we exhaust our budget. Then if you want to put some things back and get other things, we'll do that. I have all day.

"If you find something else you really want and it meets our standards, you can use your own money to buy it. I am limiting my buying this trip to only those things on our list of school needs. Megan, let's make an adult decision now to act with maturity. If there is any arguing or crying, our shopping will stop, and we'll check out with whatever we have. Will you agree to this? Do you think it is fair? OK. Then when we're finished, let's eat out together. I enjoy being with you—you're really very special to me."

Wisdom from God's Word

Differences in taste will always exist within families, especially between parents and teens. But if everyone's thoughts toward clothing and makeup are in line with God's thoughts, working with those differences should be a stretching experience, but not a stressful one.

Your beauty should reside, not in outward adornment—
the braiding of the hair, or jewelry, or dress—
but in the inmost center of your being,
with its imperishable ornament, a gentle, quiet spirit,
which is of high value in the sight of God.
1 PETER 3:3–4 (NEB)

CHAPTER 23

BIZARRE HAIRSTYLES

It's Saturday afternoon, and you're out sweating over the front flowerbeds, planting perennials. You glance down the street at a young man swaggering up the sidewalk, and shake your head in disbelief. One quick glance and you see his bright orange hair, shaved high on the sides. Feeling sorry for his parents, you hope he's not a close friend of your teenage son. As you look again to see if you recognize him, the spade drops from your limp hand as the boy walks right up to you with a wicked sparkle in his eye. "Hey, Dad. What's up?" His face grins. Your heart groans.

What Can You Do?

You need to deal with boys and girls differently. Girls from the ages of ten to eighty habitually experiment with their hair, searching for just the right look. The exercise can be valuable as they learn how to manage their hair and decide what looks most flattering on them. Since most girls are not usually out to shock people with their appearance, their experimentation is mostly benign. Although it may be disconcerting to see your daughter go from a brunette to a blonde to a redhead, it's probably best to be tolerant of her efforts. Part of her identity is finding her own look, and she can't do that if you micromanage her grooming.

The situation is different for boys. The reality is, every parent will probably have the opportunity, at some point, to scratch his head over his teenager's choices and wonder, *What on earth is going on here? I want to do what's right, but this is just bizarre.* When this happens, you need to evaluate what your reaction will be. Will you major on the majors or major on the minors? That is, in the overall scheme of things, how important is his hair? We often hear the maxim, "Pick your battles." The decision is yours: is this an issue that you really want to go to war over? Ultimately, you cannot have total control over a teenager. The whole point of this phase of life is to prepare your child to live independently of you—to prepare your "kite" for flight.

Now, I can hear you say, "There is no way my son will get any responsible job looking like this. No one will take him seriously." That may be true, but if he does not care, forcing him to change his outward appearance to suit you will not change his heart and mind. In terms of guiding principles, you can try to influence him, but you cannot control him.

- If you believe this behavior is intended to defy your authority, to hurt you, or to show disrespect for your desires, then you may think the situation warrants "going to war." You may present your son with the choice of not going out in public except to school or of shaving off the rest of his hair completely and starting over. In that case, he may resume his social life when his hair has grown enough so that he does not look like a neo-Nazi.

- A further option would be for you to keep him out of school and home-school him until his hair grows out. Your son's school may assist you here, for many schools have dress codes that prohibit extreme hairstyles. If he wants to be back in school with his friends, he may have no choice but to tone the hair down and adhere to school rules, just as he does the dress code.

- Many times, the battle ends here because all the teen wanted was to see your reaction. The hair-raising stunt may be a clumsy test not only of the boundaries you have set, but also of your character: Do you blow up, shout, threaten, and rail over the fact that he's used Kool-Aid on his head? (This is a popular method of coloring that lasts only until the teenager's head gets wet.) How do you react to off-the-wall surprises? Is his appearance more important to you than how he feels about you?

- On the other hand, you may decide that the situation does not constitute a defiance of authority, but is merely a statement of the need for attention or independence. Teenagers are often caught up with the need to belong, to do what their friends are doing. If you feel this is the case with your son, you might make a neutral comment like, "Um, that sure is an interesting hairstyle. You should get a lot of reaction with that one. Won't it be entertaining to go back and look at this year's school picture ten years from now?" Apart from your comments, chances are your teen will probably experience enough discomfort from the negative looks and comments of others that he will give it up.

What Could You Say?

In talking to him about it, you could say, "I know you think I am old-fashioned and have no concept of what is 'in.' And I know you want to make your own decisions about your appearance. I'm OK with that as long as you use good judgment and common sense. Tell me, what were you feeling when you shaved off all your hair?"

Listen carefully to what he says. He might say only, "I was just messing around." He will probably "blow it off," because that is the requisite response to anything a parent takes issue with. So you probe deeper: "Well, obviously you wanted a lot of people staring at you—that's what it will accomplish. I want to ask you something, seriously: Do you feel valued for who you are—you as a person? Do you feel valued for what you look like? In the core of your heart, do you feel that you're really worth something?"

Now you may get an "I dunno" or a blank stare. There may be little response if your question hits too close to home. Perhaps there was a time in your own life when you were struggling with a sense of self-worth. Tell him about it. This could be a golden opportunity for your son to identify with you. All young people struggle in this area. Think about a time when you were trying hard to be liked, yet the people you were trying to impress didn't even know you existed. You still may harbor some of that desire for affection and attention. We never really outgrow that need. If you could share from your own experience something you did to get affection that was either foolish or ineffective—maybe trying to "buy" a friend with gifts or wear only certain clothes—then your son can better understand why such superficial tactics don't work.

Then you could move on to say, "It's taken me a while to learn that a person's real value isn't based on performance or looks or even ability. God created you with an intrinsic value that supersedes all those things, just because He loves you so much. I know that you have tremendous value to me apart from your hair. There's no telling what God is going to do in your life, and I want you to know that I am here for you. I care about you, and Son, I'll always love you.

Now go back to the hair. "I have no desire to stop you from doing things you want to do, but with all my heart I believe that this hairstyle is not going to get you what you really want."

Wisdom from God's Word

If you want teenagers to view the world and all the people in it with the eyes of the Lord, then model His compassion before their eyes. Search out the "statement" behind any bizarre look and remember to check it out before you write it off.

The LORD does not look at the things man looks at.
Man looks at the outward appearance,
but the LORD looks at the heart.
1 SAMUEL 16:7

CHAPTER 24
BODY PIERCING

Your daughter appears at your office unannounced. "Angela! Hi! I'm glad to see you. What brings you around this afternoon?" you ask while glancing uneasily at Angela's friend Gina, whom you don't know well. All you really know about her is that she wears short tank tops, low hip huggers, and a distracting array of earrings in her ears, one in her lip, and one in her eyebrow.

"Hi, Mom. I just wanted to let you know that Gina is taking me to get a belly ring," your daughter declares. You glance at Gina's navel, which is indeed pierced, then look at your daughter in dismay. Not only has she brought reinforcements in making this request, but she has chosen to make it in front of your coworkers, knowing you would not want to make a scene.

Body piercing is one of the more extreme conflicts you may face over your teenager's appearance. *Body piercing* is more than piercing the earlobes, which is now considered so benign that some parents have their infant's ears pierced. Today, body piercing may include rings, studs, or pins piercing the lips, tongue, nose, eyebrows, ear cartilage, back of the neck, nipples, navel, or genitalia.

What Can You Do?

In the above situation, you can calmly and quietly say, "Honey, it's always good to see you, but you may not do anything until we have a chance to talk about this. Go on home, and I will see you after I get off work." Then walk away so she cannot argue.

At home, when you ask her why she wants this done, she may tell you that "everybody" is doing it. It's the thing to do. You can counter, "Not *everyone* is doing it. Not *all* teenagers do it because not *all* parents will let them do it—whatever 'it' is." (I know that if I'd had my navel pierced, I would have been banished to outer Mongolia by my father! There's no way this argument would have worked with either of my parents.)

- Now whether your teen has already had it done or is just contemplating it, and whether it involves a son or a daughter doesn't really matter. In any case, the role of parents should always be to do what is best on behalf of their children, not do what they manipulate you to do. Saying nothing is not a solution. You should do some research, first, as to public health laws in your state. In certain states, it is illegal for a minor under the age of seventeen to get body piercing done without parental consent (the age is eighteen for tattoos). Your teenager may have friends who know of shops that will circumvent these laws, but warn her that those places are unregulated by health inspectors and do not follow strict sanitary procedures. An infection that results from an unsanitary piercing can literally be life-threatening.

- Let your daughter know that you understand her desire to fit in with her group. Then say, "Help me understand why you want to do this. Do some of your friends have their bodies pierced?" If the answer is yes, then ask, "Did you like those people before? Or do you like them now only because they got this done?" Be careful not to say this in a manner that demeans her friends. The point is to help her evaluate the reason for getting pierced. Ask, "It hasn't made you like them more, has it?" You can anticipate that the response will be, "No, I already liked them." Perhaps this line of thought will lead her to admit that if she's hoping these friends will like her more because she follows suit, she may be in for a disappointment.

Guide your teen in a discussion about the qualities of real friends. Proverbs 27:17 says, "As iron sharpens iron, so one man [or teen] sharpens another." Several key points in your discussion about friendship should be:

— If you have a real friend, you'll be better. Because of that friend, you'll be sharper. Friends help refine us.

— A real friend is committed to helping you do what's best for *you*, not what everyone else is doing.

— A real friend looks at your heart, knows your need to be accepted, and accepts you because of who you are, not because you go along with the "in" crowd. A real friend would encourage you to do the right thing (for example, to keep you from being grounded, if for no other reason!).

• Refer to an adult your teenager likes. The example you cite could be your church's youth director, a favorite teacher, or a relative who has been attentive to your daughter: "Look at Dana, who is beautiful inside and out. How could her appearance be improved by a belly ring? Or Ms. Anderson, who has her own company. Can you see her fretting over a ring getting caught in her clothes? She doesn't have time." Think about another respected adult (possibly the principal or the pastor). "Do you think having a hole in his nose would be acceptable?" Then say, "Do you think it's possible that when you become 30, having a hole in your nose may not be 'in'? Then what do you do?"

• You could ask, "What if you develop an allergic reaction to the metal, or you get an infection? Are you willing to pay the medical expenses for treating it?"

This point in the conversation would be a good opportunity for you to talk about the respect your daughter should show her body as the temple of God (1 Cor. 6:19) and the right she has to demand that others respect it.

Viewing her body as a commodity to gain popularity indicates a serious problem with self-esteem.

Use this opportunity to emphasize the importance of her making decisions about her body based on what is best for her personally, not based on whether she thinks it will gain her acceptance among her peers. Girls, especially, need support in asserting ownership of their own bodies. For some girls, this is the rationale for piercing: "It's my body and I can do what I want with it!" In that case you may need to remind her of the fact that "You are not your own; you were bought at a price. Therefore honor God with your body" (1 Cor. 6:19–20).

- In many cases teenagers don't really want to have the piercing done, but the peer pressure seems so overwhelming that they can't say no. Therefore, they may be counting on you to do say no for them. A firm parental *no* can actually be a relief. Whether they let you know it or not, your no gets them off the hook and allows them to save face among their friends at the same time. Your daughter might be happy to blame you for forbidding something she secretly didn't want anyway.

If other measures fail, or you don't wish to play the "heavy" yet again, you may want to enlist outside help to provide your teen with enough moral and spiritual support to resist the temptation. Perhaps there's an older sibling whom your daughter respects. Tell the older sibling that you need help. There would be nothing more effective than an older brother coming in and saying, "You want a navel ring? All the guys at college think piercing on a girl is gross. It's a major turn-off." It's amazing what certain esteemed family members can do, whether it's a brother or sister, grandparent, uncle, aunt, or cousin. They can carry much weight within the family dynamic.

What Could You Say?

In discussing the situation with your daughter, you might say something like this: "I understand how important it is to you to fit in with your friends. But since they obviously like you already, I don't see the need to put holes in your body that ten years from now you will wish weren't there. So my answer to this request has to be, 'Definitely not.' Later on, when you become an adult, what you do will be your decision. But right now, your real friends like you for who you are, not for anything you do to your body, and that's how it should be. And believe me—sincerely—I like you too!"

Some would say this is not an issue of right versus wrong and there is no Scripture expressly forbidding it. Nevertheless, it is an invasion of the body for no good reason, and it conveys a look that others may find offensive. Ultimately, doing what is in the best interest of your teenager is the most loving thing you can do.

Wisdom from God's Word

Being accepted by our peers is important to all of us, but it is especially important to teenagers. Acceptance is often the motivation behind their choices. Likewise, it is often the motivation behind your consternation. Yet, if teenagers can stand alone, not constantly comparing themselves with the crowd, God will produce in them a sense of positive pride.

Each one should test his own actions.
Then he can take pride in himself,
without comparing himself to somebody else.
GALATIANS 6:4

Others claim the Scripture in Leviticus 19:28 forbidding the Israelites from piercing their bodies would be the biblical principle to apply here.

"Do not cut your bodies for the dead
or put tattoo marks on yourselves, I am the LORD."
LEVITICUS 19:28

CHAPTER 25
PROCRASTINATING

Once again, you find yourself in an all-too-familiar situation. You and your family are sitting in the car in the driveway with the engine running. It is hot. Everyone is grumpy. You were already ten minutes late leaving, but you have to wait for your sixteen-year-old daughter . . . as usual. You honk the horn for the fourth time, then everyone in the car perks up to see her finally appear in the doorway. But it is a false hope that you will be leaving right away, because she chirps, "Oops! Forgot my sunglasses," and disappears back into the house. You have about had it and are now convinced that something has to be done!

Procrastinating is one of those tendencies that seems to come prewired in certain kids. You will know early on if you have a procrastinator—you will be reminding her to get up, reminding her to get ready, reminding her to get her things together, and she will still be ten minutes late every time. This is also one of those problems that is made worse by adolescence, when more responsibility is resting on your teen's shoulders to get herself places on time. Perhaps she is also responsible for taking younger siblings to school, or has a job for which she must not be late. It becomes crucial for her to get a handle on this habit because when she is driving, she will attempt to make up for lost time by going just a little bit faster and taking a few more chances on the road. Accident investigators say the number one cause of traffic accidents is *excessive speed and recklessness.*

There was a newspaper article some time ago about a young woman who became a paraplegic as the result of her car colliding with another when she tried to beat the stoplight. She had been in a hurry because she was late. In the article she said something to the effect, "Every time I sleep, I dream about that accident. I relive it over and over again. I can't help it. It always ends the same—the screeching brakes, the horrible crunching, the spinning out of control. If I had only left the house ten minutes earlier, I would not have felt pressed to try to make that light. I am in a wheelchair today because of ten minutes." How do you prevent something like this from happening to your teenager?

What Can You Do?

- Chances are, your teen wants to correct this bad habit as much as you want her to. When she was younger, it may have been a way to assert control or create excitement, but now scrambling around to make up for lost time is nothing but a hassle. Sit down with her and brainstorm about what she thinks can be done. Look at her schedule—are there certain times of the day that are troublesome for her? For instance:
    - Does she need to get up fifteen minutes earlier in the morning? Or maybe she needs to shower before going to bed.
    - Is she trying to do too much before she needs to leave? See what she can do ahead of time.
    - Is she not being realistic about how long the drive takes? If the freeway is bumper-to-bumper every day, maybe she should try another route.
- It could be that you've already discussed all of this with no result—she's a piddler. She dawdles until she looks at the

clock and shouts, "Oh, no! I have to leave in five minutes or I'll be late!" If this is the case, she has to entirely relearn to pace herself. Because she paces herself by the clock, you can help by setting her bedroom clock fifteen minutes ahead. Even though you know it's set ahead, she also knows why, and the shock of seeing the advanced time whenever she glances up may short-circuit her tendency to dawdle.

- One procrastinator I know well was motivated to "get a move on it" when her roommate chose to quit waiting on her to go to various events. The time-conscious roommate got tired of trying to use anger as a motivation. (It didn't work anyway.) So she decided to maintain a pleasant disposition. She clearly communicated the time an hour ahead of time when they needed to leave. Pleasantly (for a change), she called out "The horse and buggy leaves at 9:00." Then again at 8:55, "The carriage leaves in five minutes!" And at 9:00 when Miss Procrastinator wasn't heading for the car, Miss Promptly drove away. The first time Miss Procrastinator was left behind, she was stunned. The second time—well, she was ready and waiting. (Miracles can happen . . . with the right motivation.)

If your teenage son procrastinates getting ready, he probably procrastinates in other areas as well. Long-term school projects get put off until the night before they're due; his room hasn't been cleaned in weeks (or months).

What Could You Say?

You might say, "Sean, I see you have a research paper due in four weeks. This is a great opportunity for you to practice planning ahead so you won't have to pull an all-nighter and end up feeling bad about yourself. Sit down and divide the project into phases and then figure out a workable schedule for completing each phase. I'll do my part by looking over each phase as you complete it. You can post the schedule on the fridge so we'll both know when the phases are due. You'll experience the peace of mind that comes with having a project ready on time. I'll expect the schedule to be ready by

Sunday night. If you don't have it ready by then, no TV until it's done. And the same is true for each phase. You will be amazed at how good it feels not to be stressed when you get something in on time. You'll be so pleased with yourself, you can bet your teacher will stand up and take note. Let me know if you have trouble figuring out how you want to divide up the project, and I'll be happy to help you."

Wisdom from God's Word

Habits are never easy to break. Procrastination is certainly no exception. God's Word offers a guiding principle that can help your teenager realize that doing things late is not the proper behavior from your perspective or from God's:

> *For there is a proper time and*
> *procedure for every matter,*
> *though a man's misery weighs*
> *heavily upon him.*
> ECCLESIASTES 8:6

CHAPTER 26
ANOREXIA AND BULIMIA

Something strange is going on with your daughter. Betsy is obsessing over her body. When she looks in the mirror, she sees herself as fat. Yet when you look at your precious Betsy, she seems painfully thin. Months ago, you found her vomiting after dinner. You were concerned. "I'm okay," Betsy said, "Please, please, don't worry." But you know she's not okay and now you really worry! Multiple times a day, Betsy is *bingeing* and *purging*—eating large amounts of food and then vomiting the food as a way to control her weight. Then at other times, she eats little, skips meals, or fasts. She's addicted to diet pills. She over-exercises. To your horror, you now uncover boxes and boxes of laxatives hidden in a dark corner of her closet and the light is beginning to dawn. Your daughter has an eating disorder. She's desperate to control her weight. But her control is now out of control and it could cost her her life! How can you help her stop hurting herself?

"Mirror, Mirror on the wall . . . who's the thinnest of them all?" Anorexia and bulimia are especially prevalent among high-school athletes involved in gymnastics, cheerleading, swimming, diving, figure skating, and wrestling—any sport or activity in which the ideal body shape is lean. Likewise, both male and female models, dancers, and actors are highly subject to eating disorders. The more dedicated the performers, the more compelled they are to control their weight . . . if necessary, by unhealthy means. Typically the onset of these disorders is the teenage years, when their bodies are naturally growing larger and fuller. They see themselves as fat even when they are not. Inside their hearts they feel powerless, totally out of control. But at least, the one thing they *can* control is food: how much (or little) they eat and how long they keep it down. The dilemma is that by means of anorexia and bulimia, they have *control that is out of control* . . . and it can lead to death!

"You're fat." "You're ugly." "You're disgusting." "You're worthless." "You don't deserve to eat." "You deserve to die." These are the words of a never-ending dialogue that plays over and over in the mind of a person suffering with a severe eating disorder. The inner voices encourage their victims to continue to abuse their bodies through starvation, bingeing and purging and other dangerous methods of weight control, even bringing them to the brink of death. They convince their victims that the world would be better off without them and they deserve to die. This rhetoric goes beyond low self-worth or negative self-talk. These teenagers are filled with self-loathing and self-hatred. Our accuser, Satan himself, plays the leading role in bombarding his victims with these lies of destruction. But we are told, "Be self-controlled and alert. Your enemy the devil prowls around like a roaring lion looking for someone to devour" (1 Pet. 5:8).

What Can You Do?

- First, learn everything you can:
    - *Anorexia nervosa* is a psychological disorder characterized by compulsive and chronic self-starvation—15 percent or more below one's ideal body weight—due to an abnormal fear of weight gain.
    - *Bulimia nervosa* is a psychological disorder characterized by repeated bingeing and purging episodes

due to an insatiable craving for food along with an abnormal fear of weight gain.

Hunger is not the issue here. Food becomes a substitute for intimacy and emotional filling. Then there is a compulsion to get rid of the food in order to have the "ideal body image." How? Several ways: enemas, diuretics (which dehydrate the body), laxatives, and emetics (which cause vomiting).

- Understand why your teenager feels powerless.
  - Is or was there abuse in the home? (verbal, physical, sexual, or chemical)
  - Is there excessive criticism? (an overly critical or perfectionistic parent; excessive comments about appearance and diet)
  - Are there high performance demands? (emphasizing only what they *do,* not who they *are*)
  - Was there an abortion? (guilt over taking an innocent life)
- Don't be controlling. Your teen already feels out of control. The issue for your daughter is that she is trying to feel some sense of control over her own body. Neither does it help to be overly simplistic. Saying, "Well, just stop" is not going to enable her to stop. "Shoulds" are not helpful, either, as in, "You should gain weight."
- Confront in a loving way. There is a great relief in getting a secret out in the open. Understand at the same time there can be resistance, but your daughter probably wants very much to stop such self-destructive behavior.
- Listen, listen, *listen* to what is being said. Give focused attention, looking eye-to-eye. Verbalize the love you have for your teenager, and show physical affection.
- Be honest about the dangers of anorexia and bulimia, and insist on professional help. This is not something you can conquer by yourselves. For negative reinforcement, it can be very helpful to explain the physical symptoms, while also sharing the story of others. For example, one mother whom I know received a phone call from her daughter's college friend telling them about her purging. They

brought her home from school severely underweight. The mother tried everything she could to be loving. She waited on her. She did everything she could, but nothing turned her around. Eventually she had purged so much that the gastric acid ate through the septic tank, requiring a replacement at the cost of $10,000. They didn't have that kind of money! So the young woman realized, *I can't afford this*, and she stopped. If purging destroyed a septic tank, you can imagine what it would do to your teeth or your esophagus.

— Dental problems from vomiting gastric juices. This causes erosion of tooth enamel and, therefore, many cavities as well as tooth loss.

— Irregular menstrual cycles—periods stopping for two and three months at a time. When a woman's fat level drops below 22 percent of her normal body weight, her menstruation ceases. Bulimics have irregular cycles. Anorexics' cycles have ceased. Many young women become infertile and therefore unable to have children.

— Irregular bowel movements, as the bowels become totally dependent on laxatives. (This is part of the "purging" process. For many, it's not just one laxative at bedtime, but five at one time, possibly thirty in one day.)

— Hair loss. Especially for the anorexic, there is growth of baby, almost down-like, hair on the body.

— Thyroid deficiencies as energy levels drop.

— Swelling of feet, hands, and glands due to the water imbalance. With continual vomiting, the glands beneath the jaw get swollen, and bags form under the eyes.

— Kidney failure due to dehydration.

— Disturbed electrolyte levels (of calcium, phosphorus, magnesium, chloride, sodium, and potassium). This physical symptom is the most dangerous. In your heart you have an "order" of minerals that affects the electrical charge of the heart.

Think of a cord of Christmas tree lights. The first light shines, then the second, then the third, and fourth, fifth, sixth. The correct order is essential. If one light goes out they all go out. Your electrolytes affect the electrical impulses that regulate your heart rate. With frequent purging by laxatives, enemas, and vomiting, you lose minerals such as sodium, which produces an "electrolyte imbalance." This causes a cardiac arrest (heart attack), and the final result is death. Forty-nine percent of all bulimics have disturbances in their electrolyte levels.

- Talk about emotions on the feeling level. So often there has been a "stuffing" of the emotions. A former bulimic told me that she grew up being forbidden to cry around her father. If she became emotional in front of him, he would tell her to go to her room until she could get control and then come back and talk. So she learned then that it wasn't right or good for her to express emotions.

- Don't try to force feed your teenager—"Just take a few more bites." The problem is not with the physical action of eating, it lies in her perception of herself. Shame is also counterproductive. There is no point in saying, "That's gross!" She knows it's gross, but she can't seem to help herself.

- Do stick with your child, even if there is resentment, even if there is an appearance of not budging. As Proverbs 18:24 says, "There is a friend who sticks closer than a brother." You may need to be that parent-friend. Be faithful to pray. "Pray for each other so that you may be healed" (James 5:16).

What Could You Say?

You might say, "Betsy, I love you with all my heart—you have no idea the depth of love I have for you. I am so sorry that I have not always remembered to show you how much I love you. Sweetheart, God loves you not based on what you do or how you look, and I love you just because of who you are in the way God made you. You are so significant that God has a wonderful plan and purpose for you. What you are doing to yourself right now breaks my heart on behalf of you. You are much too precious for me to stand by and do nothing while you destroy yourself this way. Please, please come with me to talk to the doctor—we have an appointment tomorrow. Please help me understand, and together we'll learn how to stop it. God has hope for you. I have hope for you. And you, too, can have hope for your heart."

A word about spiritual warfare is necessary here. If your teenager shares that she hears inner voices condemning her and urging her to continue abusing her body, pray for her.

> Dear Father,
>
> In the name of Jesus Christ, we refuse the lies that Satan and his demons keep putting in (your child's name) mind. We claim the victory that is already hers through the shed blood of Christ. Remind Satan and his demons that she has been bought and paid for by the blood of Jesus. She belongs to You. Please put a hedge of protection around her heart and mind. We especially ask that you thwart the lies of the father of lies and give her the assurance that she is loved, cherished, and precious in your sight. In the holy name of Jesus, Amen.

Wisdom from God's Word

With patience, love, and godly counsel, your teenager will begin to understand that honoring God in her body is the best thing she can do for herself.

> *Do you not know that your body is a temple of the Holy Spirit,*
> *who is in you, whom you have received from God?*
> *You are not your own; you were bought at a price.*
> *Therefore honor God with your body.*
> 1 CORINTHIANS 6:19–20

CHAPTER 27
DEPRESSION
AND SUICIDE

Scott never smiles. He comes home from school every day, goes to his room, and sleeps. He only comes out when you force him to join the family for dinner. . . . Carol seems so lifeless; she never has the energy to go anywhere or do anything. . . . Our daughter stormed out of the house last night saying, "I hate myself, I don't have any friends, and I can't stand school!" . . . Jonathan's notebook fell open on the kitchen floor last week. Dreary poems describing death and darkness tumbled out. . . . Robert had the smell of alcohol on his breath when he came home from school yesterday.

These are the comments from bewildered parents attending a Saturday breakfast meeting in the hopes of preventing another teenage suicide.

The teenage years have always been a roller coaster of mental, physical, and emotional change. And teenagers today have to confront many more challenges than finding a date for the senior prom. When the difficulties they face are surviving a broken home, navigating through the sea of available drugs, plotting a course through the plethora of pornography, escaping unwanted pregnancies through the trauma of abortion, or competing for the prize of a Princeton education . . . the days of hot dogs and summer baseball games have a nostalgic appeal.

Some depression is normal. Death, disappointment, and heartache all come with the territory of being human. If your teenager is sad or listless following some such event, be patient. Not having your experience in life, a teen faced with losing a beloved pet or getting cut from the team may react with full-blown grief. Teens are just beginning to experience the losses that are part of life. But, in time, with loving support, your budding geniuses should regain their equilibrium.

So how can you know if your teen is just deeply suffering the pangs of unrequited puppy love, or truly having catastrophic thoughts camouflaged behind eating disorders, substance abuse, social isolation, school difficulties, and yes, even overachievement? Parents must not ignore any suspicious behavior in the hope that it's "just a stage" and things will get better by themselves. You can't afford to hide your head in the sand when faced with the signs of depression, and how many teenagers will carry a sign that says "Help me, I'm depressed!"?

What Can You Do?

- First, walk through your own front door. Often the symptoms displayed in a teenager are only the reflection of stress going on in your own home! Are you struggling with marital difficulties? Does your work take precedence over your teenager? They sense when all is not right on the home front and react accordingly. Whether they deliberately seek your attention through negative behavior (rebel), or unknowingly mirror (reflect) the atmosphere of the home, remember your primary responsibility as a parent is to meet the needs of your children. Priorities, family relationships—the pain of a troubled teenager can be just the catalysis that strengthen a marriage and deepen family relationships. In the body of Christ, "if one member suffers, all suffer together" (1 Cor. 12:26 RSV).

- Because objectivity is difficult when it comes to diagnosing depression in your own teenager, search out as much information and advice as you can from teachers, neighbors, church leaders, and friends. Take your teen for a physical check-up, mentioning a concern about depression. More importantly, talk directly with your teen and compassionately discuss your concerns.

  — *Seek* conversations with your teenagers about their thoughts and feelings to *show them you care!*

  — *Share* similar experiences you had as a teenager that turned out positively to *give them hope!*

  — *Seek* professional help from a specialist in adolescents to *give them help!*

- When teenagers with severe depression do not receive help, they may turn to suicide as an escape. The four main danger signals are: (1) threats or talk of killing oneself; (2) giving away treasured possessions; (3) making a will; and (4) talking like there is no hope or no one cares. Teens with these kinds of danger signals should receive immediate help from a qualified professional.

- Teenagers need structure and achievable goals. Set up specific responsibilities and maintain accountability! When they accomplish a task, give them praise. Develop a list of healthy activities for each week. including church and a youth Bible study. They need to hear that they are an important part of the family and that their lives have purpose.

- Don't think that just because teenagers go to church and attend the youth group that they are immune from severe depression. Suicidal thinking can be a reality in any family! If you suspect your teen or someone you know is vulnerable to thoughts of suicide, don't be afraid to ask, "Do you sometimes feel so bad you think about harming yourself?" Discussing suicide openly is one of the most helpful things you can do. It shows that you are taking your teen seriously, and that you care. If the answer is yes, then follow through by asking, "Have you thought how you might do it?" If the teenager has already formed a definite plan, the risk of suicide is very high. (Never buy into the myth that people who talk about suicide don't kill themselves. Eight out of ten suicidal people speak about their intent before killing themselves). If you think there is immediate danger, DO NOT LEAVE THE PERSON ALONE. Stay with the teen until the crisis passes, or help arrives.

- Tragically, many young people feel they simply can't cope and that no one cares. But suicide doesn't have to happen. Draw a boundary line for life by presenting a . . .

  ### Contract of Care

  — Ask if the teen would be willing to make a contract with you. "Will you promise that if you are considering harming yourself you will call me before doing anything?" (If you are not the parent, give the teen your phone number.)

  — Put the contract in writing. Both of you sign the contract.

  — Make a commitment to talk on a regular basis.

  — Ask your teenager to read each day Jeremiah 29:11: "'For I know the plans I have for you,' declares the LORD, 'plans to prosper you and not to harm you, plans to give you hope and a future.'"

- Develop a trusting relationship with your teenager. Do fun things together. Share your childhood and teenage experiences, as well as stories you've heard from your parents and grandparents about their experiences. This will give your teen an understanding of the family heritage and instill pride and a sense of identity. Who your teen has come from says something about who your teen is today. Share things that will bring a feeling of pride and present a challenge at the same time. Teenagers need something to live up to, a goal to attain, a task to accomplish. Simultaneously read inspirational biographies of Christians of great faith whose lives will motivate your teen to have great faith. (Young people continually look for role models.) Give your teenager the assignment of finding something the two of you can do together that will benefit someone else. Perhaps an elderly person needs something done around the house the two of you can do together. Just as your teenager's relationship with God is vital, having a good relationship with you is also vital.

What Could You Say?

If your teenager is drowning in the darkness of depression, your words can literally be life-giving if they contain the light of hope. The apostle John wrote, "In Him (Jesus) was life, and that life was the light of men. The light shines in the darkness, but the darkness has not understood it." Use your words to help your teenager focus positively on life by focusing on The Life, "I realize you are hurting. I know how that feels because I've been there more than once myself. You think the pain will never go away. And that's what I want to help you with. The way to get away from pain is to replace it with something that isn't painful. The way I do that is by focusing on something that brings me peace or joy. That is what Jesus did when He was facing the horrible suffering of the cross. He looked beyond the pain and focused on the joy that was to come later. I want you to do the same thing.

Right now, think of something you would enjoy doing on a daily basis and begin doing it now. Do it for however long it takes for you to be engrossed in it mentally and emotionally. What would you want to do? I expect you to commit to doing it or something else equally enjoyable every day, and to tell me when you're starting and when you're stopping: I promise you that over time the pain you are experiencing now will diminish and be replaced with joy. Pray with me right now, 'Jesus, I give you my pain. Thank you for the joy you have set before me in (enjoyable thing to do). I choose right now to focus on You and on (enjoyable thing to do). I am depending on You to dispel the darkness with Your light. Amen.' Now, go on and do it. And be sure to let me know when you stop so we can talk about how it went and what you will do next in order to keep the darkness away. I love you, and I'm proud of you for taking responsibility for yourself."

Wisdom from God's Word

The mental and emotional focus of your teenager is the key that opens the door to light and life. Teenagers are not the masters of their fate, but they are to master their minds and focus on the object of their faith:

> *Why are you downcast, O my soul?*
> *Why so disturbed within me?*
> *Put your hope in God,*
> *for I will yet praise him,*
> *my Savior and my God."*
> PSALM 42:11

CHAPTER 28

SPIRITUAL DROUGHT

Your daughter is busy, busy, busy—involved in many worthwhile activities at school and church. Sherry appears to be enjoying herself, but you've become vaguely disquieted about her frantic pace—it's almost as though she's on a treadmill that she can't stop. Despite the fact that Sherry attends almost every church function, she appears to spend no time in private prayer or Bible study. When asked to say grace at dinner last night, she impatiently spouted, "Thank you God, for this food, and for—the table and chairs and all the stuff we have. Amen." She seemed to be preoccupied with superficial things, and had expressed some strange attitudes about God that made you wonder about her relationship with Him.

What Can You Do?
Church attendance for anyone is necessary and good, but just because your teen attends regularly does not guarantee a healthy spiritual life. As a matter of fact, church activities that are hectic, mindless, or strictly for entertainment can actually drain away time and energy from a teen's spiritual life while lulling him into thinking that because these activities are

church-related, they automatically count as something he does for God. And in an effort to be "hip," some youth directors encourage some pretty bizarre activities, for instance, the "Burping Contest." This was organized by one youth director for a social at a church member's house. All young people, boys and girls, drank large quantities of soda pop to facilitate burping, then staged a contest to see who could produce the loudest, most prolonged burps. Prizes were to be awarded. One participant, in going deep for the burp, instead threw up all over the host's sofa. Now this kind of activity sure wouldn't enhance anyone's spirituality, especially that of the hostess who had to clean up her upholstered furniture.

- Think of the mind as a mirror of the spirit. A person's spiritual life is essentially his thought life. How much of your teen's thought life is spent in prayer or meditation on God's Word? How much time does he spend contemplating God's purpose for his life? How much of the time is his mind cleared of clutter, waiting on God for insight into dilemmas, conviction of sin, or encouragement in trials? How much time does he spend in private thanksgiving and praise? Very little, you suspect.

- In assessing the extent of the problem, first evaluate his schedule. If he has precious little time for sleep or study, let alone prayer or Bible study, he may seriously need to pare down. If you speak to him about schedules, you need to look at your own as well. How is *your* spiritual life? Does your teenager see that spending focused time in solitude with God is important to you? Does he see that it affects your outlook and behavior? Does he see gentleness, kindness, faithfulness, and self-control reflected in your life? Most importantly, does he see God at work in your life? If your teenager sees this, he will more than likely be naturally drawn into a spiritual life of his own.

- Some parents have found it profitable to have regular, one-on-one Bible studies with their children. This should be an informal discussion time with guidance in developing Bible study skills and prayer. While he should hear you pray, you must not force him to pray. I heard about one overzealous parent who would punish his child when the boy could not think of anything to thank God for. Of course, we should teach our children gratitude, but in a way that encourages and reassures. That child, incidentally, is now a man who never prays.

Your prayer life and Bible study should communicate the following to your children:

— God is good—"For the Lord is good and His love endures forever" (Ps. 100:5).

— God loves us—"I have loved you with an everlasting love" (Jer. 31:3).

— God is powerful—"His divine power has given us everything we need for life and godliness" (2 Pet. 1:3).

— God requires our obedience—"If you love Me, you will keep My commandments" (John 14:15 RSV).

• Above all, your child should see you putting these truths to work in your own life. He should see the fruit they bear in terms of the peace and harmony and profit. If he doesn't see you applying the Word of God to your life, then what he will learn from Bible study is that only hypocrites study the Bible.

The Old Testament has a wonderful prescription for leading children into a spiritual life: "These words which I command you this day shall be upon your heart; and you shall teach them diligently to your children, and shall talk of them when you sit in your house, and when you walk by the way, and when you lie down, and when you rise. . . . And you shall write them on the doorpost of your house and on your gates" (Deut. 6:6–7, 9 RSV). When the words of God are so much a part of you that they permeate everything you do, then they will become a part of your children as well. Incidentally, a writer friend of mine took the notion to repaper her foyer with pages cut from a large old family Bible. When another Christian reproved her for desecrating a Bible in this manner, she pointed to Deuteronomy 6:9—which she had plastered right under the light switch without even realizing it at the time.

What Could You Say?

"Sherry, sit down with me for a minute; we need to talk. I want you to know how much I love you and how proud I am of you. At the same time, I'm really concerned at how you're pushing yourself with all these activities. Is all of this really necessary? How much time are you leaving yourself to just let down and think?

"I don't want you to get burned out and used up. I want you to understand the peace of resting in God. The very best way you can do this is to set aside regular quiet time and prayer. I can't force you to do that—it would be wrong for me to even try. But you've seen how much it helped me when I was going through that bad spell at work. Please think this through with me and tell me how it strikes you.

"Starting next Monday, I'd like for us to begin going through Proverbs. I'd like for us to go through the Book of Proverbs together. I'm thinking we can read a chapter a day, discuss it at night and we'll get through the book in a month. I think it also would be helpful to pick one verse a day to memorize. After Proverbs we can do whatever book you'd like. What do you think?"

Wisdom from God's Word

The key to having a full spiritual life is remaining in vital relationship with Jesus, who is the way, the truth and the life. Make certain you are fully depending on Christ Jesus as your life, and then watch your teenager follow suit.

> *No branch can bear fruit by itself,*
> *but only if it remains united with the vine;*
> *no more can you bear fruit,*
> *unless you remain united with me.*
> JOHN 15:4 (NEB)

CHAPTER 29
ATTITUDE PROBLEMS

"No, I don't have time to wash the car. Anyway, I don't feel like it. . . . No way am I going to some little kid's birthday party. I don't give a flip what his dad did for you. . . . I'll go see whatever movie I want! Quit nagging me!" It sounds as though your son has developed a real attitude problem. Andy argues with you about almost everything. He's being defiant, disrespectful, and just generally a pain to be around. Because there is very little pleasantness between the two of you, you're reluctant to spend any time at all with Andy, even though you know you should. Avoidance is obviously not the best course, but what is?

What Can You Do?
- This behavior is related to the problem of talking back discussed earlier, except it goes deeper. Because you need to break the patterns of negative interaction and attitudes that have become ingrained, begin with something positive. Acknowledge your son's desire to be treated with respect, and then make every effort to give him that respect. Likewise, state your expectation that he will reciprocate. This means that complaining, criticizing, and argu-

ing will no longer be tolerated. Should he continue to resist your authority in these ways, the consequence will be the loss of his audience. You will physically withdraw from his presence. (What fun is haranguing if there's no one around to hear it?) What you're saying by this action is, "I am not going to fight you about this."

- You also will make clear that all privileges—taking the car, going out on dates, attending parties, even using the telephone—will be on hold until the two of you can respectfully talk to each other. If "back talk" continues after you've made your position clear on a particular issue, you will not only have to put all privileges on hold, but cancel previously planned activities as well.

- If your son gets angry enough to be verbally abusive, he must make an apology. Even if he is insincere, saying the words is a lesson in humility he needs. You can't make a person repent in his heart, but your gentle insistence that he acknowledge his wrongdoing can be used by the Spirit of God to convict him privately later.

- You should look at an attitude problem as a classic cry of insecurity. Adolescent boys typically cover self-doubt or fear with a facade of aloofness, insolence, or hostility. If he feels he must act that way around you all the time, it may indicate he feels unsafe and insecure in his relationship with you—he may sincerely think you don't like him and seriously doubt that you love him. You must convince him otherwise.

- Invest time and attention in your teenager. He's worth it. Make a concerted effort to talk with him about some topic of interest—maybe a girl he likes, a course he's taking, or a sport he enjoys. Try to move the conversation from the factual level to the feeling level. Getting him to talk to you honestly is a good sign. Don't disparage what he says. You must stay on guard to prevent the conversation from deteriorating into the old patterns of criticism or interrogation that made him stop talking to you in the first place.

- Plan some family activities or one-on-one activities with your teen. Be open to including some of his friends so that you can get to know them and develop a relationship with them; your son will really appreciate the opportunity to play host. Rework your schedule to spend as much time as possible at home so that you will be available when he feels like talking. Remember to look for positive things in your teen to praise, and offer encouragement whenever possible. If you look hard enough, you *can* catch him doing something good. Snatch that opportunity for praise the moment it comes along. It's true that kids live up to or down to our expectations. In praising your son, you're telling him that you expect praiseworthy things of him.

What Could You Say?

When you discuss this wall of attitude between you, you might say something like, "I want you to know that I love you and I'm concerned about our relationship. Unfortunately, we've established a pattern of communication that is unpleasant and unproductive, and I think you would agree that it is dishonoring to the Lord. I believe that the Lord holds me primarily responsible for allowing it to get to this point. Therefore, I'm not going to engage in these shouting matches with you anymore. When we disagree on an issue, I'll just state what I believe is best for you. If you believe there's something I've overlooked, I will listen once as you present your position calmly. After hearing it, I will make every effort to make a fair decision, which I'll state *once*. I will not repeat myself or try to justify my position. I'll expect you to accept it even if you disagree with me. (If you have a disrespectful attitude, more privileges with your friends will have to be removed.) I would like to see our conversations become more positive and meaningful because I do love you and deeply want our relationship to improve." Ask him to repeat what you said to make sure he has heard you correctly.

If your teen keeps pressing you and wants to argue, then you can say, "Your actions right now leave me no choice but to withdraw privileges. I don't want to, but you're making that decision for me by your choices. How many privileges I have to withdraw is ultimately up to you."

You may discover, as you spend more time with your son, that his attitude problem is symptomatic of a larger problem, such as unhealthy interests, angry or resentful friends, a dying spiritual life, or a drug problem. Hard as it is to believe, this discovery is the beginning of healing. How to deal with these larger problems is discussed in the next chapter and in section 5.

Wisdom from God's Word

Talkative teenagers can be a blessing or a curse, depending on the talk that comes out of their mouths. As you gain mastery over your own words, speak words that build up your teenager. Perhaps you both could put this Scripture on your bathroom mirrors and be reminded.

> *Do not let any unwholesome talk come out of your mouths, but only what is helpful for building others up according to their needs, that it may benefit those who listen.*
> EPHESIANS 4:29

CHAPTER 30
OCCULT FASCINATION

Your previously well-adjusted teen seems to have morphed into another being overnight. Now Kathryn wears only black clothes and black makeup. She won't go to church anymore. Her grades have plummeted. She's sullen, sarcastic, and secretive. She is hanging out with a whole new set of friends who won't come into your home. Worse, she is preoccupied with entertainment that has dark, disturbing themes.

There will always be a curiosity about forbidden things. That natural curiosity is the hook that practitioners of the occult use to lure unwary teens. Astrology, séances, palm reading, witchcraft, goddess worship, and earth religion all make the promise of divulging hidden knowledge to their disciples—in fact, the word *occult* means "hidden." The occult describes any practice used in an attempt to gain supernatural power or knowledge apart from God. "What's so wrong with the occult?" a teen may ask. "Why are you against it?" The primary answer is, "Because God is against it." Make no mistake, involvement in the occult launches you into a realm clearly forbidden by God. (See Lev. 20:6–7.)

What Can You Do?

- First, pray for wisdom in regard to the occult and educate yourself about occultic practices and patterns. For example, the choice of clothing. One evening I was teaching on this subject and afterward, a woman poured out her distress because her daughter had begun to dress in black—only black. Her disposition had become dark. Her spirit seemed oppressed. The mother went home and insisted that her daughter get rid of the black. Then she met with several parents who also were concerned about their teenagers, and they, too, insisted that their teenagers give up the Gothic clothes and hard rock. Well, the result was fascinating. After a battle over "rights," the kids switched to C & W (country and western), and the mother later told me that over a period of time, her daughter's countenance actually changed—she was no longer as depressed and withdrawn—and that was true of the whole group.

- Don't be lulled into a false sense of security. Even if a teenager's interest in the occult appears superficial, parents need to take it seriously. Dabbling is dangerous. Casual church-going is no covering against the occult. Even teens who attend church can be at risk. They think their religion protects them when, in reality, it can be too flimsy to stand up under satanic assault. While there is positive supernatural power made available by God (see Col. 1:27), there is also the negative supernatural power that finds its roots in Satan, who will exploit any avenue that gives him influence over a soul.

- To find out what is going on with your teenager, investigate. Read the lyrics of the songs your teen listens to—typically, they are printed on the CD inserts. What is she doodling? Look inside her school notebooks or book covers for satanic symbols or emblems representing anarchy. If you see a distorted cross, it may be a depiction of the cross of confusion, of anti-justice, of Nero, Diana, or Lucifer. Most people are familiar with the swastika or the broken cross, but you also should look for the upside-down cross, the pentagram, the horn-hand, or the hexagram.

Contact ministries that deal with the occult or mysticism to learn the significance of the symbols you find. They also will alert you to other clues. Remember, Jesus said, "The truth will set you free" (John 8:32). Song lyrics or written works that deal with destruction invert the truth and enslave those who listen. Therefore, if you find something that is obscuring or perverting the truth of the cross, you need to deal with it immediately.

- Get help from people you know who have a deep understanding of spiritual warfare—perhaps your pastor or other church members. Ask them to begin waging war on behalf of your teenager. Be wary, however, of those churches that do not teach about spiritual warfare. They won't be able to help you. Remember, when you're dealing with the occult, you're dealing directly with the enemy of our souls.

Initially, seek to gain the cooperation of your teen in ridding your home of all occultic objects: CDs, trinkets, occultic games and the like. Even items of astrology. Years ago, I had a cup with signs of the zodiac given to me as a gift—a cup just the perfect size to hold pencils. Then I came into an understanding about the occult, but I didn't want to discard the cup—and it became a major internal battle. But then I thought, "If I can't be faithful in the little things, how can God trust me with the big things!" I knew I had to throw away the cup. If your teenager does not see the need to get rid of the occultic objects, explain that the mere physical presence of such objects is in opposition to God and gives Satan entrance into your home, thus exposing everyone who lives there to demonic influence. What's more, since your home is dedicated to the Lord, who saved you, your admittance of His enemy is an insult to Him.

Acts 19:19 reveals that those who formerly practiced sorcery brought out their occultic materials and burned them. To enable your teenager to experience deliverance from the grip of darkness, you *must rid your home of anything occultic* that sets itself up against God.

- Learn to answer the major questions your teenager may likely ask. Many people, even Christians, don't know what the Bible says about the occult. For example:
    - "What's wrong with seeking help to communicate with a loved one who has died?" This practice is not only forbidden by God, but it also opens the door to being defiled by demons. Leviticus 19:31 says, "Do not turn to mediums or seek out spiritists for you will be defiled by them."
    - "What about astrology and horoscopes?" The Bible gives the answer in Jeremiah 10:2.
    - "What about magic charms protecting me?" The Bible gives the answer in Ezekiel 13:20.
    - "What about nature worship?" The Bible gives the answer in Exodus 20:4–5.
    - "What about witchcraft?" The Bible gives the answer in Micah 5:12.
    - "Why is it wrong to consult the dead in behalf of the living?" The real problem is that people involved in the occult look to a "practice" apart from God for supernatural knowledge—ultimately this is a misplaced faith that God absolutely forbids. "When men tell you to consult mediums and spiritists, who whisper and mutter, should not a people inquire of their God? Why consult the dead on behalf of the living?" (Isa. 8:19).

What Could You Say?

In broaching this subject, you can tell your teen, "I have some questions for you. Can a light switch be on and off at the same time?" You may get a confused look, but the answer is no. "Can something be dead when it is alive?" No. "Can something be true when it is a lie?" No. "Can something be both good and evil?" All of these answers must be no. "Can you handle fire with your bare hands and not get burned? Can you scoop up water and not get wet?" Your teen will get the point.

Then you ask, "Can you open your mind to evil and not have that evil influence you? Can you be a child of God and

Satan both? I'm really concerned about the interest you have developed in something very dangerous. I love you too much to see you sucked into self-destruction. With all my heart, I want you to experience the joy and peace of a life that is pleasing to God. Let's see what we can do about this together, OK?"

Wisdom from God's Word

Curiosity kills more than cats; it kills many teenagers who dabble in the occult not knowing it brings darkness and death. God's Word is clear about the dangers of the occult with its many deceptions.

Woe to those who call evil good
and good evil,
who put darkness for light
and light for darkness,
who put bitter for sweet
and sweet for bitter.
ISAIAH 5:20

SECTION 5
SOCIAL BOUNDARIES

Here is where the rubber meets the road.
Your parenting will be most severely tested as your
teenager enters the center stage of "socialization." Now
you can see the reason Jesus instructed us to pray,
"Lead us not into temptation, but deliver us from evil"
(Matt. 6:13 KJV). Pray this on behalf of your teenager
who will need all the help possible to stay out of
temptation's way. Let's talk about the times they don't.

CHAPTER 31
REFUSING EXTRACURRICULAR ACTIVITIES

Your son, who never gives you any trouble, starts refusing to participate in any group activity. Although he is good at basketball, he wouldn't consider trying out for a team. He likes to play chess, but only online. Heaven forbid that he actually meet with a bunch of people to play. Scouting is out—he refuses to wear a uniform. In fact, it seems that he has an excuse to avoid joining any organization, and you are concerned that he's missing out on something that could be important to his life.

This problem may seem a rather antisocial beginning for the section on social boundaries, but the reasons for such reluctance are so diverse that it's actually a good introduction. In general, sports, clubs, and organized volunteer activities are valuable opportunities for social growth, especially for teens. They help build social skills, physical skills, confidence, and camaraderie. Occasionally, however, a teen simply refuses to participate in any organized activity.

What Can You Do?

- Pray you will be sensitive and discerning regarding the reasons for your teen acting this way. Has he always been somewhat reclusive? The jolt of entering adolescence may make him retreat even further. Has he always been self-conscious? His sudden physical changes may make him cringe at the thought of running onto a field under the scrutiny of hundreds of eyes. Is he afraid to try new things? Is he afraid of rejection? Does he insist everything be done his way? Is he sensitive to criticism? Your teen may not tell you the real reasons for his reluctance. He may not be fully aware of them himself. You'll have to dig and deduce to find them, but it's important that you do, and not just lay down an ultimatum that he participate or else.

- If the reasons amount to immaturity or fears that your child can overcome, then you have more work to do. Investigate the group activities offered through your child's school. Belonging to a group gives him an identity at school, friends with common interests, and a reason to look forward to the school day. Try to persuade him to join a group on a trial basis. Resort to rewards, if necessary. One mother of a shy, withdrawn girl offered to buy her an expensive pair of jazz shoes if she would take dance class in high school. This led to a place on the drill team and, later, a leadership position.

- Unfortunately, some kids feel so disenfranchised from their school, and some schools are so mercilessly controlled by cliques, that your teen may feel it is impossible to fit in. The next step is community groups. See if your son will run an Internet search on topics that interest him, or send him to your local librarian for help. Whatever field he finds—robotics, philately, trebuchets—there's going to be a group somewhere for him to try on for size. Obviously, you will not drop him off just anywhere, but go with him until you are satisfied that the group is a healthy outlet for him. Then keep abreast of his activities and accomplishments.

There are few things sadder than a child pursuing competence in a stimulating field of which his parents are totally ignorant.

- It may be that after all of your research, encouragement, and trial runs, your child's activities fall off again until he is back to spending most of his time in his room. In this case, you need to know exactly how he is occupying himself. If it's reading, find out what kind of books he enjoys and guide him to appropriate material. If it's writing or drawing, ask to see his work. Some kids who have deep, introspective minds and a creative bent simply need a lot of time alone to nurture their gift. If this is what your son is doing, you will recognize it by the quality of material he turns out.

Some kids who are truly called of God to a special purpose will feel the need to cloister, to spend a great deal of time alone wrestling with their God-given purpose, seeking understanding and strength from Him. If you see that your child is truly marching to the beat of a different drummer and needs silence to hear the far-off music, you would be wise not to interfere.

What Could You Say?

"I know God created you for a purpose and I want to do all I can to help you develop His purpose. What do you want to be in life? And what are you doing to develop the talents and interests God has given you? I know that God has made you special and unique, and I wouldn't want to change you for anything in the world. But I do feel responsible to help you develop to your full potential, and I'm concerned about your lack of desire to be a part of any group activities. There are great benefits to be gained through group interaction. Can you explain to me why you are not interested? Take some time to think about it. Let's pray about what gives you the greatest sense of joy and fulfillment. Then let's plan a way to develop your potential. We'll pray about finding just the activity that rings your bell!"

Wisdom from God's Word

Make a concerted effort to interest your teenager in nurturing friendships. Share the importance and benefit to you of your friends, as well as the story of David and Jonathan. David's son Solomon wrote these words about the importance of friends.

Two are better than one,
because they have a good return for their work:
If one falls down,
his friend can help him up.
But pity the man who falls
and has no one to help him up!
ECCLESIASTES 4:9–10

CHAPTER 32
REFUSING CHURCH PARTICIPATION

Your otherwise pleasant teenage son suddenly decides that he doesn't want to go to church anymore. Since you insist Ronnie go, Sunday morning has turned into a battle of wills that ruins the sanctity of the day. "I have friends who don't go to church," he snaps back. "Are you saying that none of them have any moral character? They are better people than everybody in the church!" Ronnie's refusal distresses you, knowing he needs biblical morality and Christian character—he needs Christ now more than ever. But Ronnie is adamant that he does not want to go and will not go.

What Can You Do?

- First, it's important to talk to your teenager to find out what, exactly, is the problem. There may be a good reason your son does not want to go. Is the youth group boring? Is the teaching irrelevant or unbiblical? Is there a problem with gossip or bullying? Ask about the youth group. Is it "alive or dead"? Is there true Bible study?

Ask what is the real reason he doesn't want to go to church.

- More alarming, is someone at church making your boy uncomfortable? Much as we would like to believe the church—any church—is a safe place for our children, Scripture warns us that emissaries of Satan can worm their way into otherwise good churches (see Rev. 2:14, 20). And newspaper headlines about church leaders who are forced to resign under the weight of evidence of impropriety are distressingly frequent. So the only way for you to really know what any particular church group is like is to go yourself. It may be that a change of churches is in order.

  You may find it helpful to come right out and ask, "Has anything ever happened at church or with anyone from the church where you found yourself sexually pressured or morally compromised? Do you know of any sexual abuse? Are you uncomfortable being around anyone?" Obviously, if the answer is yes, get the details and report it immediately. Those issues being directly addressed, most likely the real reason for the rebellion is an issue of the heart.

- If you are satisfied that the problem does not lie with the church, then it's time to tactfully talk to your teen. Don't be dictatorial, self-righteous, or legalistic about your teen attending every church function, but help him prioritize which activities are the most important.

- Many a teenager has been reached through parachurch organizations—Christian camps, Young Life, Youth For Christ, choir and mission tours, youth Bible studies, Christian volunteer organizations. Pray that your teenager would develop strong friendships with authentic believers—wise Christian friends who will sharpen him and make him wise. Proverbs 13:20 says, "He who walks with the wise grows wise."

At one point my father forbid Mother and the four of us children from going to church. I was sixteen at the time. The year before we had joined a vibrant, biblically based church, and I genuinely believe my father felt the church was competition to him.

Although my mother was typically a tenderhearted, submissive woman, on this one point she did not yield. She negotiated that she would stay home with him, but we children had to be in church. She believed with all her heart that she would be failing as a parent if she didn't prioritize the training we would get at the feet of wonderful Bible teachers. The words she used with me were, "When you are raising children, church is a non-negotiable. Children will be taught values that will last a lifetime. And of greatest importance," she said, "they must come to know the Lord." Nothing was more important than experiencing a life-changing relationship with Jesus. I thank God for a mother who numerous times took the heat to prioritize what was truly best for us.

What Could You Say?

Years ago when I was a youth director, I gave many parents a logical, practical approach for how to talk with their teens with tact. Before you meet with your teenager, pray for God to prepare his heart and to speak through you "A wise man's heart guides his mouth, and his lips promote instruction" (Prov. 16:23).

Practice this approach:

- "More and more, I'll be giving you greater freedom to make your own choices, and one day you'll be out on your own, making all of your own decisions."
- "But for now, God has given me the privilege of having you under my protection and direction."
- "Do you want me to try to do what is pleasing to God?" Wait for a response. It should be affirmative.
- "My highest priority is to please God, especially where it concerns you."
- "Because I deeply love you, I want to please you too. However, I know there will be times I can't do both."
- "In this case, it would be wrong for me to say you don't need to go to church. The truths that are taught there are going to be crucial to you, especially when you're out on your own. You know, God will hold me accountable for how I raise you."

- "Let's both go to the services, learn as much as we can, and pray that we'll come away with at least one truth we can put to good use during the week. OK?"

Wisdom from God's Word

Sometimes the purpose of going to church is obscured by the routine practice of going to church. If your teenager is balking at continuing "the practice," do your part to make sure your church is meeting the purpose that Paul outlined:

Let us not give up meeting together,
as some are in the habit of doing,
but let us encourage one another—
and all the more as you see the Day approaching.
HEBREWS 10:25

CHAPTER 33
BROKEN HEARTS

Your precious son, the apple of your eye, is crushed. Devastated. Inconsolable. Despite the fact that he is the most attractive and intelligent young person around, he has been cruelly rejected by the object of his affections. The fact that he is not yet permitted to date is no deterrent to heartbreak because crushes can begin in kindergarten. But when his attention is not reciprocated, the last thing he wants is sympathy from a parent.

What Can You Do?
- Unrequited love is probably a tragedy in every teenager's existence. (Remember your first heartbreak?) Don't ignore it or dismiss it as "puppy love," because while it may be a small thing in the grand scheme of things, to your teen it *is* ruination! If you can't show understanding in what you consider the little things, your son will not trust you with the big things. Therefore, have a strategy ready. Distractions are good; extra time with other people whose company your teen enjoys is especially profitable, as is helping someone in need. Your teen will benefit from

focusing on giving to someone else, as Acts 20:35 states, "It is more blessed to give than to receive." And there is a saying, you can't spray perfume on someone else without getting some on yourself. Avoid shopping trips or piling on special foods—this only encourages the association of emotional comfort with spending money or eating. A little extra attention from you could never hurt.

- Be lavish about calling your teen's attention to his desirable qualities. He may protest, "Aw, Mom, of course you think I'm cute. You're supposed to say things like that," but say it anyway. Mention even more things that are attractive about him, especially good character qualities. Even if he acts like he's not listening, he is.

- Keep in mind that broken hearts have inspired some of the most famous art and music in history (as well as the entire genre of country-western music). Encourage your own suffering artist to pour out his thoughts and feelings on paper. He may discover an aptitude he never guessed he had. One fourteen-year-old boy lamented in verse:

    He doesn't think it's at all important,
    For love is just a thorn,
    All alone he walks the path,
    One plus none, you do the math. . . .

    He filled a whole notebook documenting his feelings, which certainly gave him something to look back on years later. One mother I know cherishes a watercolor painting of a drooping hibiscus her daughter produced in the throes of rejection. The painting is special to the mother not because it is a reminder of a painful incident but because she has seen how God has poured out love and affirmation on her daughter in the intervening years.

    Resist platitudes. Telling your daughter, "Oh, you'll get over him" may prove true eventually, but it's not helpful now. Acknowledge that she is really hurting and enter into the pain with her. You can probably dredge up a traumatic incident or two from your own history to share with her. It may amaze her to discover you were once a teenager and survived. But it will encourage and comfort her. Just holding her and crying with her may be the best thing you can do for her. Remind her that Jesus' sufferings make it possible for Him to identify with her. Likewise, her sufferings will enable her to identify with and offer comfort to others. God will not waste her pain, but He plans to use it to increase her compassion and give her a ministry in the lives of others. Suggest she memorize 2 Corinthians 1:3–4 which says, "Praise be to the God and Father of our Lord Jesus, the Father of compassion and the God of all comfort, who comforts us in all our troubles, so that we can comfort those in any trouble with the comfort we ourselves have received from God."

Be careful not to disparage the heartbreaker, even if you think he is scum. You are permitted a certain bemusement as to why he would act this way, but do not let her get anywhere close to the idea that people have to react to her the way she wants. This could set her up for a lifetime of frustration. Besides, the time will come when it's your child doing the heartbreaking. One day you will ask, "What happened to Brendan? I never see him anymore." And she will say, "Oh, we decided to see other people." If she's not crying when she says this, then you know there's probably a broken heart at Brendan's house. Let her tell you what she wants, but don't probe if she's not ready to talk.

* A word of caution. Don't get over-involved. You don't know the whole story. One mother explained the circumstances of her daughter's breakup with a prominent man's son: "It was general knowledge that they would get married. But she began feeling he was totally dominating her and making physical demands beyond her comfort level. When she finally got the courage to break up with him, no one could believe it. Everybody thought he was the greatest guy. The whole church was talking about the breakup because the boy was going around crying to everybody who would listen about how she broke his heart. People started looking at her like she was the villain in all this."

So, take the high road. Teach your teen to look past disappointments. As she has the opportunity to see you look for the good in each day, she will learn to do it too.

What Could You Say?

If your teen does give you an open door, take the opportunity to communicate that you care. You might say, "I'm so sorry you're hurting. I know you are trying to rise above it and act like you're OK, but it is OK to grieve. God gave us tear ducts just for times like these. Even though tears will not change everything, they will release some of the pain you feel. Your mother and I feel your pain, too, and we want you to know we love you and are here for you."

Wisdom from God's Word

In seeking to comfort and help heartbroken teenagers, don't forget the blessed benefit of your prayers. Weep with them and pray for them. There is only One who is always close by and only One who can restore a crushed spirit.

The LORD is close to the brokenhearted
and saves those who are crushed in spirit.
PSALM 34:18

CHAPTER 34

UNKNOWN FRIEND'S PARTY

Friday afternoon, your son calls you at work: "Dad, can I go to a party tonight at Chad's?"

"Chad? Who's Chad? I don't know him," you respond.

"Oh, he's this guy at school. Please? All my friends will be there—Seth and Danny and Jarrod—you know them; they're OK. Please? I need to know now so I can get a ride with Seth. I've done all my chores and you said you were really proud of me for making an A on that physics test. Please, Dad?" You really want to make the right call here. But who is this Chad?

What Can You Do?

Here is one Kansas family's experience, related by the dad: "Our second son was eager to try out his expanded social life in the eighth grade by asking our permission to attend a friend's party one Friday evening. My wife and I asked, 'Are the parents there?' and our son automatically responded, 'Yes.'

"After dropping him off at the friend's house, we began to have doubts about the level of supervision at the party. We decided to call the house. A young girl answered, and I asked to speak to the mother. I heard her ask away from the phone, 'Does anyone have a deep voice?' Another girl got on the phone and made a lame attempt to sound like an adult. I hung up, looked at my wife, and we both said, 'We're going over there.'

"We arrived at the house only to spot our son 'making out' with a girl right in front of the living room window. We rang the doorbell, collected our son, and quickly exited with one upset and hurt young man in tow. After that incident, he realized that we meant business concerning his social life. He spent the next weekend at home, and for the next six months we confirmed all of his information with parents."

- To avoid having this happen in your family when your teen wishes to attend a party, you might start by having him get a responsible adult on the phone who knows the parents of the teen who is having the party. Get what preliminary information you can about the family's values and lifestyle. In addition, many high schools offer some kind of a *Parent Pledge*. This is a contract parents have the option of signing that states they will permit no alcohol, smoking, or drugs at teenage parties in their homes. Students whose parents have signed this pledge are highlighted in the student directory. This gives you a quick and easy reference, and it is a positive place to begin your investigation.

- The next step is to call the home where the party is taking place and speak with at least one of the teen's parents. Do not take the boy's word for it that the party will be chaperoned (would he tell you if it weren't?). Your son should understand in advance that if you cannot get one host parent on the phone before the party, he can't go. Next time, he'll give you more notice. Talking with a parent will give you a clear idea of their sense of responsibility. It may be embarrassing, time-consuming, and inconvenient to ask all these questions, but it may spare you the greater embarrassment, time, and inconvenience a large number of parents experienced recently.

    You could specifically ask:

—"Will you be there for the party?"

—"Will you be there the entire evening as a chaperone?"

—"Will there be any other adult chaperone?"

—"Will there be any alcohol available or allowed?"

—"Will you be taking responsibility for what goes on?"

How well I remember a seventh-grade party at Button's house. (Button was a smooth talker—even for seventh grade—and he knew how to "put the make" on the girls.) About an hour after everyone had arrived, Button's mother and father slipped out—all by design of course—and the bar was open with every kind of imaginable drink. (A tidge stronger than "Shirley Temple" drinks, needless to say!) I'm sure his parents thought they were being cool, but as parents they were irresponsible. Kids were all through this house as well as outside on the front lawn making out. Just because you assume parents will be present for a party at their own home, as the old saying goes, "It ain't necessarily so."

By the way, I never told my parents. Although I never would have told my father, I think I might have told my mother . . . if she had truly probed. Then we could have role played how to handle the same uncomfortable situations. Consider asking your teenagers questions when they come in from a party. Ask for them to check with you before they go to bed. That way you will find out not only if they made the curfew, but also if they are acting irrationally or have alcohol on their breath.

Some months ago several hundred parents were called in the middle of the night by the police to come pick up their teenagers at a suburban Dallas warehouse. These teens had been busted at a keg party where there was so much alcohol, they had one keg for every three people. All of the teens apprehended at the warehouse were charged with underage drinking, and a few of those over twenty-one were charged with providing alcohol to minors. All parents had to post on-the-spot bail of several hundred dollars and sign an agreement to appear in court before they could take their children home. Moreover, because the suburban school district has a zero-tolerance alcohol and drug policy, the students faced disciplinary action ranging from suspension to expulsion, depending on the severity of the charge and the students' records. One of the police officers interviewed at the scene said in disgust, "Not one of these parents knew where their kid was tonight. Well, now they know."

- You should have an understanding with your teen regarding the ground rules for his being able to attend parties. Then follow the rules you have set down, even if it means he can't go. But don't make him feel like a martyr to your rules. Brainstorm with him about alternative entertainment with other friends or family members.

What Could You Say?

You might say, "I understand how much you want to go to this party since your friends will be there, and I want you to be able to have a good time too. So, I need you to take the initiative in getting one of Sean's or Jarrod's parents on the phone, whichever one knows the family situation of the boy giving the party. After that conversation, if I like what I hear, then I'll need the phone number of the boy's parents, and I'll find out what I need to know about the party from them. After that, you and I will talk about what I've learned and make a decision as to whether it's a good idea for you to go or not. If it works out, great. If it doesn't, then maybe we can figure out something else that would be fun to do. If you want to have some friends over here, I'll provide the pizza."

Wisdom from God's Word

It requires strength of character and a cool head for a teenager to heed the warning in his spirit and say no to a fun time with the "in" crowd. Sometimes danger can be seen, and some-

times it can only be felt. In either case, share with your
teenager the wisdom of not proceeding when danger signals:

The prudent parent sees danger and gives refuge to his teen,
but the unwary lets him go and suffer for it.
PROVERBS 22:3 (PARAPHRASED)

CHAPTER 35
QUESTIONABLE FRIENDS

Your daughter has begun to associate with kids whose attitudes concern you. They are doing poorly in school. They wear extreme, antisocial clothing and hairstyles. They are secretive about their activities, and when they do come by your home, it's only to collect your daughter, Clare, and take off again. Their parents, wherever they are, appear to exert little authority over them, and these kids seem to be encouraging Clare to defy your home rules. You're very much opposed to your daughter identifying with such a negative group.

What Can You Do?
- You may want to plan a conference with your daughter. On a day when you both have plenty of time, sit down with her and gently probe for insight into her new friends. What are their families like? What do they like to do? Why do they like to present such an extreme appearance? What does your daughter think she can offer these kids—and what do they offer her? You must not be accusatory or inquisitorial. But if you ask questions in order to understand, she may open up to you about the reasons for her choice of friends.

- Plan opportunities to be with your teen's new friends, and get to know them personally. See if it is possible to develop positive relationships with them. Whenever you are around them, be friendly and non-judgmental. Find whatever ground you can for connecting with them, whether it's computers, creative efforts, or ideologies. You may be surprised at how well they respond to you. Often, teens who have hostile relationships with their own parents can form good relationships with the parents of their friends. All teens appreciate friends—and need mentors who care, even if they're old fogies. You may never know how profoundly your kindness could affect them for good. View this as an opportunity for ministry. It could change the course of their lives.

- Avoid preaching. Don't browbeat your daughter's friends with your faith. Jesus said, "All men will know that you are My disciples if you love one another" (John 13:35)—not if you win arguments about the Bible or demonstrate how morally superior you are. Ask God to reveal their needs that He can meet through you, then look at them as potential brothers and sisters in Christ.

- If your daughter has a romantic interest in one of these young men, then you will need to use even more tact. Prohibiting her from seeing him could make him all the more attractive to her and provide greater incentive for her to defy you. Instead, let her see you reach out to him, and then be reasonable about their relationship.

- If it is your son who is attracted to a girl of questionable character, you have the opportunity to exert far more influence than you realize—if you choose to. Mothers, restrain your dislike for the brazen hussy who is trying to corrupt your handsome, upright son—and welcome her with open arms. Encourage your son to bring her into your home rather than just out on dates. Be warm and courteous. Smile and converse. Say nothing remotely critical. Then one of three things will happen:
    — You will win her over with love.
    — She will get disgusted with your lifestyle and leave.

— Your son will decide he can do better and break off with her.

Any of these options is better than what you are likely to achieve with frosty disapproval.

I will never forget one woman I met at a conference where I was speaking on forgiveness. During the question and answer time, this mother shared about her son. As a young man, he began living an immoral lifestyle with a young woman who was just as carnal as they come. This unmarried pair was living in a place that didn't even have shower facilities—they had to come to his parents' home to bathe.

As deeply grieved as this mother was by her son's choices, and as upset as she could have been at the sight of this "temptress," this vixen, she could have locked her heart's door and frozen the couple out. But she didn't. Her attitude was that of rare Christlike love. She reached out not just to her son but especially to the young woman. She looked beyond her fault and saw her need. She needed the Lord. Periodically the mother gave her small gifts with Scripture verses attached. She had them over for dinner and kept her door open to them. She lived out the love of Jesus who said, "Love your enemies."

Eventually, this mother's love won the young woman to the Lord. And in time, the son followed suit and became a Christian. With that, they got married and committed their home to the Lord.

- Use the get-togethers you and your daughter have planned with her friends to draw out their positive, likeable attributes—some are there, though you may have to dig deep for them—and build from there. While you are building relationships with her friends, you are automatically supervising their activities and incurring your daughter's gratitude. If your house becomes "the" place to go, then you know, with little effort, where your daughter is and what she is doing. Just don't get lulled into complacency so that you habitually leave them undisturbed in a separate part of the house, or you may be unpleasantly surprised to find out why your house has become "the" place to go.

What Could You Say?

You might say to your daughter, "I know other people may be somewhat leery about your friends, but I really would like to get to know them for myself and give them the benefit of the doubt. I'd like for us to plan a time when we can get together with them, put out some snacks in the den. Because you are a level-headed girl, you like people for a reason, and I want to see the same things you see in them. Anyone who is important to you is important to me. So, what do you think we could plan that they would enjoy?"

It may be that after everything you try, you discover one of the group to be an incorrigible liar, abusive of your trust, or possessing the conscience of a split pea. It could be that the group is carrying on activities in your own home against your wishes. In that case, you are justified in telling your daughter, "I gave Paul every chance I could, but it seems he's mostly interested in trying to play me for a fool. I'm not a fool, and I love you too much to let your life go down the tubes with his. His choices have left me with no other option but to say he's no longer welcome in this house. I will continue to ask God to bring good into his life, but I can't see any good in your continuing a relationship with him." If you have been sincere in your efforts up until now, your daughter will understand. She may even be indignant at Paul's duplicity.

Wisdom from God's Word

Friends are vital to teenagers. Who those friends are is even more vital. Help your teens learn the importance of choosing wisely the company they keep . . . their influencers, their molders and shapers.

> *"Bad company corrupts good character."*
> 1 CORINTHIANS 15:33

CHAPTER 36
STEALING

Your son hurriedly exits your bedroom as you enter the door-way. Glancing back at Randy in concern, you walk over to the dresser where you left your wallet. Opening it, you discover the twenty dollars earmarked for dinner that night is gone. With a sinking heart, you hear the front door open and close as Randy leaves. You feel betrayed. You expect that someone may rob you outside your home, but not someone on the inside. How can you ever feel safe? You didn't actually see the theft, and you have no real proof. You know he took the money and that this will only get worse, but your sorrow is making it hard to confront the situation.

■

What Can You Do?
- Stealing takes many forms. The three different scenarios that follow, all drawn from real life, involve stealing. In the first case, a mother was repeatedly faced with the situation above. After thinking it through, she felt that it was unfair to accuse her son of stealing without proof. Therefore, one evening she carefully counted the money in her wallet, marking every bill with a ballpoint pen. Days later, when

she came up short again, she confronted her son. First, she told him exactly how much she was missing and described the marks she had made on the bills. Then she demanded he empty his pockets. When she checked his money and showed him the marked bills, he admitted he had taken them.

This boy had other, deeper problems stemming from his poor relationship with his father, problems the mother could not address by herself. Confronting him with the stolen money, however, gave her the justification she needed to insist he come to counseling with her. The boy agreed.

- If you feel you can effectively handle the problem on your own, you might consider enforcing the biblical punishment for stealing. With incontrovertible evidence or a confession of how much your son stole, he would be required to pay back double the money to the victim (see Exod. 22:4, 9).

- The second scenario involves a temptation that snares many children, not just teens. Let's say you find some clothing in your daughter's room that still has security tags attached to it—a dead giveaway that it was stolen from a department store. Since actions are motivated by wants or needs, first ask the Lord for wisdom as to what is behind your daughter's actions. If your daughter is stealing, what is motivating her?

- Confront her with the evidence, and listen to what she says. Can she produce a receipt for the item? No? If she claims that someone else gave it to her to hold, you might remind her that receiving stolen goods is also a crime. In the spirit of fairness, check out whatever she says by talking to the person she claims gave her the item. If your daughter did steal it, the truth will soon come to light.

I empathize with this situation because I remember the time I stole a candy bar from a store. When my mother saw the chocolate on my face, she walked me back to the store where I had to confess to the manager. I was deeply humiliated. It was a lesson I will never forget.

That was years ago, when I was a small child. Today the ramifications of a teen shoplifting are considerably more complicated. Store losses from theft have become so great that many stores have policies of automatic reporting of any shoplifting case to the police, no matter how minor, no matter if it's a first offense. Nonetheless, that must not deter you from taking your daughter back to the store to return the item.

- Most likely, the police will be called. Your daughter may be arrested and booked, depending on the value of the item and the disposition of the store manager. If its value is minimal, and it is a first offense, she may receive a ticket and a fine—which she, of course, will have to pay herself. She also may be assigned to probation or a first-offender program, which if satisfactorily completed will allow her criminal record to be expunged when she turns eighteen. All this is frightening talk for parents and teens to hear, but it is mandatory that you cover these consequences with your teen from the moment she is first able to shop. For a crime such as stealing from stores, whatever negative consequences you would impose will likely be secondary to the laws already in effect.

Your daughter still should apologize to the victim for her crime. This may be a condition of probation; even if it is not, an apology makes a difference to everyone involved. Of course, the item must be returned to the rack if it's still in good condition—if not, she will have to pay for it. Make it clear to her that whenever people steal from a store, they are stealing from everyone who shops there because theft drives prices up. If there was an accomplice, that person will need to be forbidden from seeing your daughter.

It's vitally important not to cover up the incident, no matter how expensive, no matter how embarrassing. Do not rescue your daughter from the consequences of her decision to shoplift; that would simply teach her that she can shoplift with impunity.

- When the legal conditions have been satisfied, you should require that your teen decide on specific ways to regain your trust in order for her privileges to be restored. Also, plan ways for her to earn money to buy certain things she wants in the future.

- In our third true scenario, a mother got into her car early one morning and, turning the ignition key, was blasted by heavy-metal music from the car radio—obviously the radio dial was not on her usual station. She then noticed the seat was pushed way back. Her son is over six feet tall and did not have his driver's license. By now quite suspicious, she checked the gas gauge and found it a quarter tank lower than it had been when she had parked the car the night before.

- In this situation, the first course of action is to calmly confront the most obvious suspect.

Should your teen already have his license when he takes your car out for nocturnal joy rides, explain to him that because he's been untrustworthy, you can't allow him to use the car for whatever time frame is appropriate given the circumstances. Tell him that you look forward to his earning the privilege to be able to drive again soon. Emphasize how much you want to trust him and delineate what privileges and freedoms he can earn by being trustworthy. Then be sure to reward him for keeping to the boundaries. (But, in any case, hide the car keys at night!)

What Could You Say?

If your son confesses, you can proceed with a heart-to-heart conversation with him. If he refuses to confess but there is no other explanation, you can still say: "Teddy, I know how excited you are about cars and the idea of driving. And I know it's going to be fun for you that whenever you are able to drive legally, you won't have any reason to panic when you see a patrol car. It will be good for me as well—I will have lots of errands for you to run. But you can't drive yet, and I'm very hurt and disappointed that you would break the law and betray my trust by sneaking out with the car. If you're stopped by the police, the ticket you receive will cost you several hundred dollars, and you will have to pay it. I will not. If you have an accident, that could cost thousands of dollars because you are not covered on my insurance policy. And because you are driving illegally, we could be sued by anyone you hit.

"What's more, any of those consequences would delay your getting your driver's license for a very long time. Therefore, the car is strictly off-limits, and because you chose to jump the gun on something that requires a great deal of maturity, it's clear that you're obviously not ready to handle the responsibility of driving. Consequently, we're putting off getting your license for an additional six months. And if I find that you defy me on this again, you won't get your unrestricted license for another whole year."

Wisdom from God's Word

God desires to take your teenager from stealing to giving, and He plans to do that through putting your teenager to work.

> *He who has been stealing must steal no longer,*
> *but must work, doing something useful with his own hands,*
> *that he may have something to share with those in need.*
> EPHESIANS 4:28

CHAPTER 37

SEXUAL ACTIVITY

Karen has been spending a lot of time with Neal, her boyfriend. Way too much time. You've caught them in compromising situations. You've lectured and grounded her, but your daughter continues to see him. You suspect much more is going on that she doesn't want you to know about. You feel deeply frustrated, concerned, and fearful about your daughter's physical and spiritual state.

This has got to be one of the most difficult areas in dealing with your teen, especially if it gets to the point that you have to come out and ask, "Are you having sex?" When I was a youth director right out of college, I heard through the grapevine that one particular boy from a good family was sexually active with a girl in our group. Now what was I to do with that information? Should I say something to the parents? Should I talk directly to the boy? I had not been around this boy very much and did not feel close enough to him to ask such a personal question, but I knew that his parents were conscientious, deeply committed Christians. My thinking was, *If I were a parent, I would want to know so that I could help my child,* and I really believed these parents would do that.

It was very uncomfortable for me to tell them what I had heard, but I did. I emphasized that this was something I did not know firsthand, but they might want to talk to their son about it. The parents approached him, and he admitted that he had been involved with the girl. That confrontation, because it happened early in his life, had a positive, profound impact on him.

Deep within the heart of every parent is this fear that their teen will lose control to the hormones that are kicking in, especially when peer pressure is escalating and the influence of parents is lessening. I think that's why 2 Timothy 2:22 carries such an impassioned plea: "Flee the evil desires of youth"—don't just walk away. Face it, teens can be self-indulgent. They typically have a temporal value system—they're not looking at the long-range impact of their actions.

What Can You Do?

- Now, if you've waited until your son or daughter is a teen to talk about sex, you're about eight years too late. I suggest that when they are about five years old, before they hit first grade, you should begin to teach them what boundaries they need in regard to their bodies. You should instruct them, "The part of your body that is covered by your bathing suit is private. No one should touch that part of your body, unless it's the doctor, until marriage."

  One Texas mother explained, "When our son was seven, my husband explained the facts of life to him, knowing that children today encounter sex in school very early. We've also taught him the biblical view of sex and how harmful secular values are. Now, at thirteen, he knows about sex but he's not jaded." It was also her opinion that "parents who want to save their children from premarital sex and its inevitable woes but who watch trashy TV and movies are shooting themselves in the foot."

- Some Christian parents get a jump on potential problems by restricting their teens' dating and encouraging them to "court" instead—rather than allow their teens to get into compromising situations by going out one-on-one, the parents make sure there are plenty of supervised group activities for their teens to get to know and interact with interesting members of the opposite sex. Church youth programs serve the purpose of giving kids a controlled environment in which to practice what they have been learning about how Christian men and women relate to each other. Then when they are older, they are allowed to date those whom they feel might make a good marriage partner. These boundaries encourage teens to look to the future when considering relationships and avoid getting into situations they are not mature enough to handle.

- Being too strict in this area can backfire, however, as one Illinois family discovered. The parents were raising their nephew, whom his surrogate mom described as "an exceptional student, very gifted, and a very respectful young man." He had been forbidden to date, but at the beginning of his senior year of high school, he made a confession. The mom related: "He said, 'Remember when you said I couldn't have a relationship with Tracy?' 'Yes,' we hesitantly answered, not knowing what would come next. 'Well, we didn't stop seeing each other, and we are still going out with each other. My conscience was getting to me, and I felt I should tell you.'

  "My husband and I looked at each other in a bit of shock. This meant that he had had an 'undercover' girlfriend for a year and a half! My husband is the kind of guy who doesn't like to be duped, but he maintained his composure very well. I, on the other hand, was worried about what other 'announcement' might be following. But that was basically all he had on his conscience, so we sat and talked peaceably through the situation.

  "As a result, we softened our position on dating. We had been quite strict about 'no dating' because of all the right reasons: it's not biblical . . . courting is a better way . . . why put yourself in compromising situations . . . keep yourself pure for the woman you are going to marry. . . .—all of which are worthy Christian ideals. However, we also saw that while he didn't argue any of those points, there were factors in his life that should have been addressed. For instance, his relationship with this girl was quite tame by today's teen standards. They had been in band together throughout their high school years and did not see each other often outside of school.

"Given his good attitude and the fact that this girl had just left for college, we decided to make allowances for them, one of which was that his girlfriend would be invited over to do things with our family when she was home from college for breaks or weekends. At this point we discovered that, due to our previous restrictions, she was scared to death of us and thought we didn't like her. This was quite funny to us because we were actually quite fond of the girl!

"Well, after our nephew called her to tell her that he was allowed to date her openly, she broke up with him one week later."

- For some families, for some reason, the safeguards have not worked. One Memphis woman who married a widower with a teenager encountered great resistance when she tried to rein in her sexually active stepdaughter: "It was a constant battle to see what she could get away with. I felt like she was flaunting her freedom in my face—'You're not my mother, and you can't tell me what to do.' I love my husband, but he just folded here. He didn't know how to handle her, so he left it totally up to me.

"First thing, I had to get his backing to set new ground rules. Number one: no boys in her room—period. She had been taking her boyfriends upstairs to her bedroom and closing the door. We put a stop to that. If she tried to take them upstairs, she lost the privilege of having them over at all. Number two: no staying out till all hours. We made her abide by a curfew for the first time in years; and if she didn't make it, we took her car keys. Number three: she had to go to church with us. She resisted this almost more than anything, but if she didn't go she got grounded from doing something else she wanted to do.

"I'm not going to tell you that these rules made her stop having sex. But they let her know we were not going to tolerate it under our roof. The following year she went to college, and we got a reprieve. She has since graduated, and I'm happy to say that our relationship is better than it has ever been. She's never said so, but I think she appreciates what I was trying to do."

- Before you approach your teens about this, educate yourself on how to talk with them. For example, one organization in Dallas, Texas, called Aim for Success has received national recognition for their work in helping teens deal with the pressures of sexual involvement. Contacting a group like this, or a counselor who specializes in family issues, can help you get the facts about teen sexuality, such as the statistics regarding the rate of venereal disease among teenagers. This kind of straight talk can make your kids take seriously a call for abstinence until marriage.

- Because girls become sexually active for different reasons than boys, you need to talk to each differently. For girls, it is an emotional matter. They feel an aching need for affection and warmth, and for affirmation that they are desirable. They also crave attention from males, so any girl who does not have a strong male presence in her life is likely to be vulnerable to any man who looks at her twice. In fact, the best deterrent to a sexually active daughter is a father who makes her feel loved.

  You also need to be aware that girls who have been sexually abused tend to fall into a pattern of promiscuity. If you know or suspect that your daughter is promiscuous, ask her about the possibility of childhood sexual abuse toward her. Do not turn away from the answers, no matter how unpleasant. The Lord brings healing, but only when the truth is brought to light. The truth sets us free!

- A boy's sex drive, in contrast, is purely physical, powered by the rush of testosterone that floods his system at puberty. He seeks physical gratification, and most guys want the reputation of being "studly." The statistics about disease and pregnancy rates should have more effect on him (in his clearer moments) than on a girl. Still, the best preventive for either is alert supervision. Chaperoning has never gone out of style.

- If there has been a breakdown of safeguards for your teens somewhere along the line, it's time for a talk. Listen to them. You might ask, "What do you think about kids being sexually active today?" Don't be afraid of piquing their interest by asking. I guarantee they have opinions about it. Don't overreact to what you hear. Allow your teens to freely express their personal views on sexual issues. Then come back and ask them for the basis for those views. Listen carefully to the process by which your teens make decisions.

If a pregnancy results from your teen's experimentation, you will need legal counsel to determine the rights (and responsibilities) of the father and the rights of the grandparents in your state. Paternity should be legally established with a blood test. You also should be aware of the limits imposed on abortion: In some states, for instance, a doctor cannot perform an abortion on a girl who is under eighteen without the consent of a parent or guardian at least forty-eight hours before the procedure. (In a medical emergency, no one's consent is required.) A girl can circumvent this requirement by getting a court order saying that she is mature enough to make the decision on her own, or that she is afraid of her parents. Then the court will appoint a lawyer and a guardian (who may be the same person) to represent her, and everything about the matter is kept secret.

Since you do not want the situation to deteriorate to this point, you must remember not to berate or condemn. God can redeem any situation, and you may find this a turning point in your relationship with your child. Choices cannot be undone, but blessings are still to be had. Consecrate the new life to God and go forward from there.

What Could You Say?

If your teenagers' views are different from yours, instead of just saying, "You're wrong," you could say, "Well, this is what

I believe," or "This is how I see it." Explain your position on sexual activity outside of the boundary of marriage, including the reasons for your position. To your daughter, you might explain, "You know, guys get real possessive sometimes, and girls can easily get trapped into thinking that in order to keep a boyfriend, she has to do whatever he wants. But God did not intend for you to be the property of any guy who comes along. People are not possessions. Your body belongs to God, and He wants you to keep it in pristine condition to give to your husband someday in a permanent, lifelong marriage relationship. (Point out 1 Cor. 7:3–5 if she doesn't believe you.) God loves us even when it feels like nobody else does. I want you to act on the fact that you are too valuable to Him to give yourself to somebody outside of marriage. I want you to demand respect for your person."

In conversing with your son, be sure to share the responsibilities that go along with being sexually active with another person, such as the possibility of his paying child support for eighteen years for a baby born outside of marriage. Don't just focus on the negatives of premarital sex; affirm the joy of a satisfying sex life in a committed, permanent relationship. For example, you might point out that no one wants to be a divorce statistic, yet those who have premarital sex are far more likely to get divorced than those who wait for marriage to consummate the relationship. While you could talk about boundaries in terms of limiting the time that your teen spends with a particular person, you should also discuss the boundary God has set. To make the point, you could write out 1 Thessalonians 4:3–4, for your teenager: "It is God's will that you should be holy; that you should avoid sexual immorality; that each of you should learn to control his own body." Ask your son to commit to reading a chapter a day from the Book of Proverbs. Have him write out all the verses that refer to sex. (He'll see warning after warning!)

You could tell your son, "God made your body, and in His eyes it is good. Now I know that I can't control what you do with it, but I can't help but feel a strong interest in your choices. After all, I've been sheltering and feeding that body—a lot—for years now, and it's been my joy to do so. But as you reach adulthood, I have to turn over that responsibility to you. I just want you to recognize the God-given worth of your soul, apart from your manhood. God has made it clear to me through His Word and my own experience that sex outside of marriage has some major pitfalls. It never pays what you expect, and it robs you of the joy of experiencing sexual fulfillment with your wife alone. I realize that your own life experience may not have convinced you of that yet, so you're left to decide whether you or God knows more on that score—and whether you trust Him or your hormones. In the right context, sex is good. It's wonderful. It's a beautiful gift for expressing love and intimacy and commitment. And it's the means by which life is conceived, which is also a gift from God. So don't use it lightly."

Wisdom from God's Word

A sexually active teenager with untamed desires can be like an untamed bronco in a corral—full of energy but nowhere to go. When taking a bronco out of a corral, you use a bridle and blinders to direct the bronco's attention to the open gate and then guide him to pursue freedom beyond the gate. As you talk your teenager out of the corral of illicit sex, direct attention to God's Word in order to go God's way. Then guide your teenager to pursue freedom through a godly lifestyle.

Flee the evil desires of youth,
and pursue righteousness, faith, love and peace,
along with those who call on the Lord out of a pure heart.
2 TIMOTHY 2:22

CHAPTER 38

DRUG OR ALCOHOL ABUSE

One evening, a man in a sports coat comes to your door. Flashing a badge at you, and identifying himself as a narcotics detective, he says your son Sammy was pointed out as a known user. Surely this can't be! You have been a responsible parent. You've made it very clear to your teenagers the boundary drawn in your home against use of tobacco, drugs, or alcohol. Yet this detective wants to talk to him about his supplier. After conducting his interview with your uncooperative son, the detective leaves. And you're left with a feeling of doubt, defeat, dejection, and a thousand unanswered questions.

How sad that even in Christian homes the best of kids can succumb to this temptation at one time or another. A major goal of parents is to prevent it from happening in the first place, but if it does happen with your child, you can take some small measure of comfort in having been made aware of the behavior before it proved fatal.

In most cases, the discovery follows a general pattern: the parents helplessly watch as their child is transformed by a sudden personality change, a precipitous drop in grades, truancy, and association with known substance abusers. Parents who see these signs are justified in searching rooms and personal effects. Once the child is confronted with the evidence, strict ground rules must be set in place. If that doesn't work, a treatment program may be necessary, and the battle for restoration may take years.

For the vast majority of people who get into trouble with substance abuse, alcohol and tobacco are the gateways. They are legal for adults, socially acceptable (to a degree), and dangerous enough to have a very seductive and glamorous allure to teenagers. But their illegal use by teens has been proven time and again to lead to the use of illegal drugs.

What Can You Do?

- Because, in your home, the reward for responsible choices and actions is an increase in freedom, it only follows that the repercussion of irresponsible choices and actions is a decrease in freedom. Once you know the situation under which your teen is using these substances, you must limit his freedom in those situations. For example, if your teenager is drinking only with certain people, then you need to eliminate contact with those people. If the behavior happens only in certain places, then you stop your teen from going to those places. If you can't do that, then readjust your schedule so that you go with him.

- It must be said again that parental example is the most powerful tool. It's much harder for the parent who smokes to tell his son that he can't smoke. They need to ask themselves, "Do I really want to saddle my son with this expensive, unhealthy habit? Is my addiction more important to me than he is? For his sake, I *quit*." Be an inspiration.

  Along the same lines, how well stocked is your liquor cabinet? How accessible is it to your kids? Please do not imagine that they (or their friends) do not know where you keep the key. For parents who think it is all right to let their kids have a drink now and then, the law disagrees. Just be aware that in Texas, if you allow their underage friends to drink in your house, their parents can have you arrested, and I know many parents who would do just that. One mother was so infuriated when her thirteen-year-old daughter told her that her best friend's parents gave them both champagne on New Year's Eve, she prohibited her daughter from going over to their house again. She said, "Maybe I'm overreacting, but I just don't trust them anymore. The girl is welcome over here."

- If you don't know the level of your teen's involvement in drugs, then you need to do a lot of digging to find out the extent of the experimentation. Explore the logic and motivation. Was it pure curiosity? Was it social? Was it the threat of humiliation if they didn't participate? The way you talk to your teen is vitally important. Open communication is essential for you to assess the situation and determine what course of action to take.

- Your teen needs to hear your unequivocal support of the laws against drug use. Without bashing him over the head with Scripture, explain the biblical principle of submitting to the authorities as explained in 1 Peter 2:13. This may be controversial, but I know parents who have called the police when their teenagers would not respect their clear-cut directive that drugs were not allowed. In one particular situation, the police came, the daughter was taken to jail, and the parents refused to bail her out that night. Did that ever make an impact! Does it work in every situation? No. If the teen's level of defiance has reached that point, there are some deep-seated issues that won't be easy to resolve. But it will work with many.

- If you are afraid your situation may come to this, calmly communicate that your teen must respect you on such a crucial point, or you may have to resort to the last-ditch tactic of calling the police. This should not be done as a power play; it should be done with a heart that is grieving. Your teen *should see that you agonize over it.* If you need to involve the police, your teenager needs to see that he has forced your hand—if he chooses the action, he chooses the repercussion.

What Could You Say?

Make it clear that you can't control your teenager's life, but you want to trust him to make the right choices. You can say, "The best thing you can do for yourself is make choices that will leave the doors of your future open to you. Each negative choice—and this particular one is a doozy—slams a door shut that may never open again, no matter how badly you desire it. If you fry half your brain at seventeen, what are you going to be like at forty? If you flunk out of school for drinking, then you've locked yourself into a minimum-wage job for the rest of your life. Are those the dreams you have?"

Research the effects of drugs; pray for wisdom as a parent, and pray that the Lord would prepare the heart of your teenager to hear the truth about what he is doing to himself. Then sit down with your teenager and present your findings.

"I hope you know how much I love you. It hurt me deeply to find out what you've been doing when you go out. Sure, I disapprove, but mostly I'm scared for you. I know I can't control what you do, but I must ask you to take a long, hard look at what you're doing to yourself. I'm not saying this to restrict you; I'm saying it to protect you. I know part of the reason you're doing this is because of your friends. I want you to have friends, but this group isn't doing themselves or you any good. Do they know the effects of what they're using? Let's look at this." Then you pull out the chart at the end of this chapter that lists the damaging effects of numerous drugs. Go over that list with him, beginning with tobacco.

Tobacco has been the drug of choice for adolescent rebellion—at a high cost. Far more than fifty thousand Americans die each year from chronic lung disease. Another four thousand Americans die each year from cigarette-caused fires. More than $30 billion is spent annually on health-care problems related to smoking. Eighty-five percent of those who experiment with cigarettes will become addicted to nicotine. Some are addicted after smoking only five to ten cigarettes. Eighty-one percent of those who smoke will experiment with marijuana, whereas only 21 percent of nonsmokers experiment with marijuana.

A former White House drug chief reported that teens aged twelve through seventeen who smoke are twice as likely to use alcohol, nine times as likely to ingest depressants and stimulants, ten times as likely to smoke marijuana, and fourteen times as likely to use cocaine, hallucinogens, and heroin as kids who do not smoke.

Tobacco releases many carcinogenic chemicals into the blood stream, the brain, and the central nervous system. It increases the blood pressure, causing the heart rate to escalate up to 40 percent. Prolonged use can lead to several types of cancer, especially lung cancer, mouth cancer, and jaw cancer, particularly with chewing tobacco.

In regard to marijuana, tell your son how 70 percent of marijuana users progress to other drugs, while 98 percent of teens who do not smoke pot do not take other drugs. Today's marijuana can be up to 20 times stronger than the plants of ten or fifteen years ago. Marijuana has more carcinogens than tobacco. It destroys brain cells; damages short-term memory retention; and causes lethargy, personality change, and decreased attention span. It also damages the immune system—someone who is a regular pot smoker is likely to get sick more often than someone who doesn't smoke pot. It produces a severe strain on the cardiovascular system, raising the heart rate as much as 50 percent. It decreases motivation and can reduce reaction time as much as 40 percent, which makes a stoned driver as dangerous as a drunk.

If your son hasn't heard enough yet, talk about inhalants: sniffing glue can impair judgment, causing a loss of self-control that leads to violent behavior. There can be suffocation and long-term brain damage. It affects the central nervous system and can even cause death.

Walk your teen through the effects of cocaine. It is highly addictive, especially in the form of crack. Once the euphoria wears off, the emotions plummet. Users are often suicidal, exhibiting violent behavior. This highly dangerous drug disrupts the brain's control of the heart and respiration, causing angina, heart palpitations, arrhythmia, and even death.

Next, discuss stimulants or uppers. These are more accessible to kids because they are sold as appetite suppressants. That doesn't mean they are more safe, however. They can produce tremors, loss of coordination, skin disorders, hallucinations, delusions, paranoia, permanent brain damage—and even death due to heart failure or stroke.

Then there are downers, or barbiturates, and tranquilizers. These can cause respiratory depression, coma, and death, especially when taken with alcohol. Many movie stars, such as Judy Garland, were victims of the deadly combination of alcohol and barbiturates.

When you have discussed all this information with him, place a hand on him and pray for his healing, for his peace, and for wisdom for both of you as you work together to get him back on the right road.

Wisdom from God's Word

Peer pressure among teenagers is tremendous and can be used both constructively and destructively. Challenge your teenagers to model Christlike character. They can influence others to do the same. Remind your teenagers they can either cause others to stumble by their compromises or keep others from stumbling by their convictions. Ultimately God holds us all responsible for our choices.

It is better not to eat meat or drink wine
or to do anything else that will cause your brother to fall.
ROMANS 14:21

What Drugs Really Do for You

Young people are under increasing pressure to try tobacco, alcohol, and other drugs. Unfortunately, the vast majority of teenagers do experiment with these substances, and many suffer the devastating effects of addiction. We adults often think that drug abuse will never touch our children, much less us. Statistics tell us otherwise: NO ONE is safe from drugs. Both we and our young people must become aware of the dangers of drugs up front. If you care about your kids, tell them the truth.

Drug Name	Drug Classification	Desired Effect	Damaging Result
Tobacco (cigs, smokes, butts, cancer sticks, coffin nails, puff snuff)	Toxin	Relaxation	Loss of appetite, addiction, cancer (lung, jaw, and mouth), birth defects, increased blood pressure and heart rate, dependency
Alcohol (booze, juice, sauce, brew, vino)	Depressant	Intoxication, sensory alteration, anxiety reduction	Toxic psychosis; brain, stomach, and liver damage; fetal alcohol syndrome; dependency; addiction; blackouts; aggression; depression
Marijuana [Cannabis—concentrated resin called hash or hashish] (pot, grass, dope, weed, homegrown, sinsemilla, maui-wowie, reefer, J. Thai sticks, joint, herb, roaches, indica, smoke, mary jane, bugs, bag, dime, quarter, Acapulco gold. THC)	Depressant, hallucinogen	Euphoria, relaxation. increased sensory perception	Cancer, bronchitis, conjunctivitis, birth defects, brain cell destruction, gateway to other drugs, immune system damage, cardiovascular system strain, alters mood, inhibits motivation, impairs short-term memory, hampers concentration, dependency

Drug Name	Drug Classification	Desired Effect	Damaging Result
Amphetamines (uppers, ups, speed, crank, white crosses, dexies, bennies, crystals, Rx diet pills)	Stimulant	Alertness, energy	Dependency, malnutrition, stroke, delusions, hallucinations, paranoia, toxic psychosis, violence, depression, skin disorders, ulcers
Non-prescription stimulants (speed, ups, uppers)	Stimulant, decongestant, appetite depressant	Alertness, energy, weight loss	Same as amphetamines plus hypertension, heart problems, anxiety, headaches
Cocaine (coke, rock, toot, blow, snow, pearl flake, girl, doing a line, lady, baseball, crank)	Local or topical anesthesia	Stimulation, excitation, euphoria	Malnutrition, depression, violence, convulsions, nasal injury, heart attack, seizure, psychosis, stroke, brain damage, dependency
Cocaine free base (base, freebase, crack, rock, C, dynamite, snorting)	Local or topical anesthesia	Shorter and more intense cocaine effects	Weight loss, depression, agitation, hypertension, hallucinations, psychosis, chronic cough, tremors

Drug Name	Drug Classification	Desired Effect	Damaging Result
Barbiturates (bluebirds, barbs, tooies, yellow jackets, blues, downers)	Sedative hypnotic	Anxiety reduction, euphoria	Severe withdrawal, dependency, possible convulsions, toxic psychosis, birth defects
Methaqualone (ludes, 714S, sopors, blue/red devils, yellows, candy, rainbows, Q's, downs)	Sedative hypnotic	Euphoria, aphrodisiac	Coma, convulsions, insomnia, severe anxiety, dependency
Heroin (H, junk, smack, China white, black tar, harry, horse, brown)	Narcotic (opiate) analgesic	Euphoria	Addiction, constipation, loss of appetite, heart disease, congested lungs, abortion, birth defects
Analogs of synthetic narcotics (China white, synthetic heroin, MPTP, MPPP, PEPAP, ecstasy, MDA, MDMA, Eve, MMDA, MDEA, XTC, TMA, STP, PMA, DOB)	Narcotic (opiate) analgesic	Euphoria, exhilaration	Addiction, MPTP-induced Parkinsonism (uncontrollable tremors, drooling, impaired speech, paralysis), permanent brain damage

Drug Name	Drug Classification	Desired Effect	Damaging Result
Morphine (white stuff, M, morf)	Narcotic (opiate) analgesic	Euphoria	Addiction, constipation, loss of appetite, nausea, organ damage
Codeine (schoolboy)	Narcotic (opiate) analgesic	Euphoria	Addiction, constipation, loss of appetite, nausea, organ damage
Methadone (dolly)	Narcotic (opiate) analgesic	Euphoria, opiate withdrawal symptom prevention	Addiction, constipation, loss of appetite, nausea, organ damage
Inhalants (solvents, glue, transmission fluid, correction fluid)	None	Intoxication	Impaired perception, coordination, and judgment; dependency; heart failure; suffocation; toxicity
Nitrous Oxide [laughing gas] (gases, whippits, nitrous, blue bottle)	Inhalation anesthetic	Euphoria, relaxation	Kidney or liver damage, peripheral neuropathy, spontaneous abortion, violence, nausea, vomiting
Amyl and Butyl Nitrite (liquid incense, poppers, room deodorizer, rush, locker room, snappers)	Vasodilator	Exhilaration	Damage to heart and blood vessels, may aggravate heart problems

Drug Name	Drug Classification	Desired Effect	Damaging Result
LSD (acid, LSD-25, blotter acid, windowpane, named after pictures on paper, mesc)	Hallucinogen	Insight, distortion of senses, exhilaration, mystical/religious experience	Intensified existing psychosis, panic, confusion, paranoia, flashbacks. organic brain damage. strong psychological reaction, impaired judgment
Mescaline [peyote cactus] (mesc, peyote, peyote buttons)	Hallucinogen (milder than LSD)	Same as LSD	Same as LSD plus extreme mood swings, distortion of senses and perceptions, deep depression
MDA, MDE, MDMA, MMDA (love drug, ecstasy, XTC, X, Adam)	Amphetamine-based hallucinogen	Same as LSD	Same as LSD plus neurotoxic sense of distance and estrangement, anxiety, catatonic syndrome
Psilocybin (magic mushrooms, shrooms)	Hallucinogen (milder than LSD)	Same as LSD	Same as LSD plus sleeplessness, tremors, heart and lung failure
PCP (crystal, tea, THC, angel dust)	Dissociative anesthetic	Distortion of senses, stimulant	Psychotic behavior, violence, coma, terror, psychosis, convulsions, impaired judgment, dependency

THINKING
OUTSIDE THE BOX

Innovative, creative, imaginative. These descriptive words seem to be part of the package necessary for great parenting. There is a very real problem with the self-proclaimed experts who say this is "the way" to deal with teenage difficulties. They present their one-two-three approach of discipline because that is what helped in their own home.

Let's face it. Every teenager is different, every parent is different, and every home is different. That's why it's vital for you as a parent to learn to "think out of the box."

Last week on a flight to North Carolina, I was seated next to a delightful woman in her seventies. As we struck up a conversation, I quickly discovered her to be a warm and winsome lady who had overcome many obstacles in life. She told me her husband left her when their children were young, and she was faced with raising several children alone.

"What helped you the most?" I asked.

"Oh, my faith," she replied. "I couldn't have done it without the help of the Lord." She went on to say her most difficult time came when one particular son became disrespectful in his teenage years and soon began hanging out with the wrong crowd. When he was about sixteen, he decided he was tired of his mother's constraints, so he moved out to get an apartment with his band of undesirables.

One day she got a call from the police, who told her that one of the boys her son was living with had been arrested for stealing. The police also confiscated a quantity of stolen goods found in the apartment. "Ma'am," the officer said, "we know your son wasn't involved in the thefts. But, since he's hanging out with this kid who is such a bad influence, would you like us to keep him in jail overnight just to teach him a lesson?"

"Will he be in a cell with dangerous inmates?" she asked.

"Oh, no," he replied. "But he will be within earshot of some pretty rough language."

"All right, then," she said optimistically. "I'll pick him up tomorrow." That night she prayed and prayed that the Lord would use this experience for her son's good.

The following morning she did several errands and basically took her time about picking up the son. Intentionally, she didn't arrive at the jail until after lunch.

"When they let him out of the cell, he just ran up and hugged me. 'Oh, Mama, I'm so sorry,' he said. 'I want to . . . Mama, I really want to come home. Will you let me come home?' I replied, 'Yes, of course, you can come home,' and I want you to know, we had no more problems after that."

I smiled and thought to myself, *here is a woman who has lived out the heart of James 5:20: "Whoever turns a sinner from the error of his way will save him from death and cover over a multitude of sins."*

This wise mother's approach is an illustration of what I call "thinking outside the box." A very perceptive single mother allows her son to experience just enough of a repercussion for breaking a boundary. In doing so, she gave him a glimpse of his destiny . . . a dismal destiny if he continued walking down the destructive path he was on. The repercussion of "tank time" gave him some greatly needed "think time."

Recently I asked a friend to do a search for the phrase "thinking outside the box" on the Internet. She discovered it was associated with words like innovative, creative, imaginative, original, ingenious, and inspired. Since I had not thought of how I would define the phrase until I arrived at this last chapter, I find some of these words helpful for communicating what I hope you take to heart from this book. Remember, boundaries are not only external limits with negative consequences for your teens. The goal of boundaries is to build inner character, and inner character produces trustworthiness. And what is trust but the major bonding ingredient of a relationship?

I encourage you to become innovative as you begin to "think outside the box" when your teens need a little internal motivation to do what is right! Get inventive and imagine ways that will lead your teenagers to not only view, but welcome discipline as the loving hand of God. As a skilled surgeon uses a scalpel to cut away that which brings physical death and to repair injuries to the body, so the Lord uses discipline to remove sinful attitudes that bring inner death . . . death to relationships . . . and to heal injuries to the soul and spirit.

That recent encounter with the mother on the plane brought to mind an incident I had completely forgotten. My own sweet mother was a number-one ace in handling difficult situations when we were teenagers. She *definitely* acted outside the box.

As a freshman in high school, I was not yet allowed to date and had very little experience with boys. One evening I answered the phone and heard this deep baritone voice telling me he was a senior at a local school. I asked how he got my number, and he said he was just dialing random phone numbers. His voice was so intriguing we talked for awhile. He called back several times, and then he wanted me to meet him after school one day the next week. He was a good deal older than I, and giving no thought to how dangerous this could turn out to be, I agreed to meet him the next Tuesday.

Though I was flattered with the attention, I didn't share my secret with anyone until the night before. From a well of inner excitement, I told my grandmother about the covert rendezvous planned for the next day. And as the school day was drawing to a close that Tuesday afternoon, I was summoned from my classroom early and told my mother was here to take me to a 3:00 P.M. dentist appointment. I was totally stunned. Mother had not mentioned anything about a dentist appointment on that Tuesday. As we drove away from the school parking lot, not a word was said about the secret rendezvous I was missing, nor was there any hint of disapproval of me in her spirit. We never talked about the incident, but I knew then Mother was drawing a boundary. She did it in a very ingenious way . . . without even mentioning my grandmother or letting on that she knew anything of my intentions. If she had "informed me" that I most certainly could not meet my mystery date or "belittled me" for being so naïve, I would have resented it, felt shamed, and been upset with Granny to boot. To the contrary, as we drove off in the car, I knew my mother loved me! Her intervening boundary did not anger or alienate me. It quieted my soul.

Ready or not, eventually the day comes for every parent to let go. No matter how adequate or inadequate you feel about the way you've done your job of parenting, one day you will wake up to find yourself retired . . . or fired! Many parents identify this milestone as the day their teenagers leave home—to go to college, start a full-time job, or get married.

Whether or not you can pinpoint that particular day when your "kite took flight," be at peace—even when it seems your child's life is not sailing on the course you would have chosen. You may not have a hand on the string, but there's Someone who does and He can do a better job at steering than you. Never give up on the innovative, out-of-the-box things God will be doing to shape, mold, and propel your kite into a "high flyer."

This is a good time to pray.

God, I've done all I can, but I know You are
still at work in my teenager's life. Since Your
love is greater, stronger, and more enduring than
mine, I am trusting You to complete what You
began when You gave me this image bearer. I'm

willing to put the future of my child into Your hands because You have declared, "'For I know the plans I have for you,' declares the LORD, 'plans to prosper you and not to harm you, plans to give you hope and a future'" (Jer. 29:11).

I've saved this little story to share with you in closing this book because it's the most original example of "thinking outside the box" I have ever heard, and it's too hard to resist laughing at it one more time. The story was in the September 6, 1998, *Dallas Morning News*.

Alan Cost could have just suspended his son's driving privileges after the boy got his third speeding ticket and stayed out way too late. Instead, he suspended his son's pickup truck—in a tree. Mr. Cost used a backhoe to hoist the back end of 16-year-old Stephen's 1986 Chevrolet pickup truck several feet in the air and used a chain to suspend it from a tree in front of their house along one of the Birmingham suburb's busiest roads. That was on Aug. 29, and it'll stay there, where all of Stephen's friends can see it, for another week or so, Mr. Cost said. There's a sign in the vehicle's window: "This is what happens when a teenager does not mind." And in smaller letters it says: "May be for sale." Mr. Cost said: "I hate being that rough on the boy, but if he ain't going to listen to me, I have no other choice."

I can hear all of you who are parents of teenagers applauding.

Do not despise the LORD's discipline
and do not resent his rebuke,
because the LORD disciplines those he loves,
as a father the son he delights in.
PROVERBS 3:11–12